Markus-Michael Müller is an assistant professor of Latin American politics at the Freie Universität Berlin. His work has focused on transnational security governance, postcolonial state formation, and the urbanization of neoliberalism. He is the author of *Public Security in the Negotiated State: Policing in Latin America and Beyond* (2012).

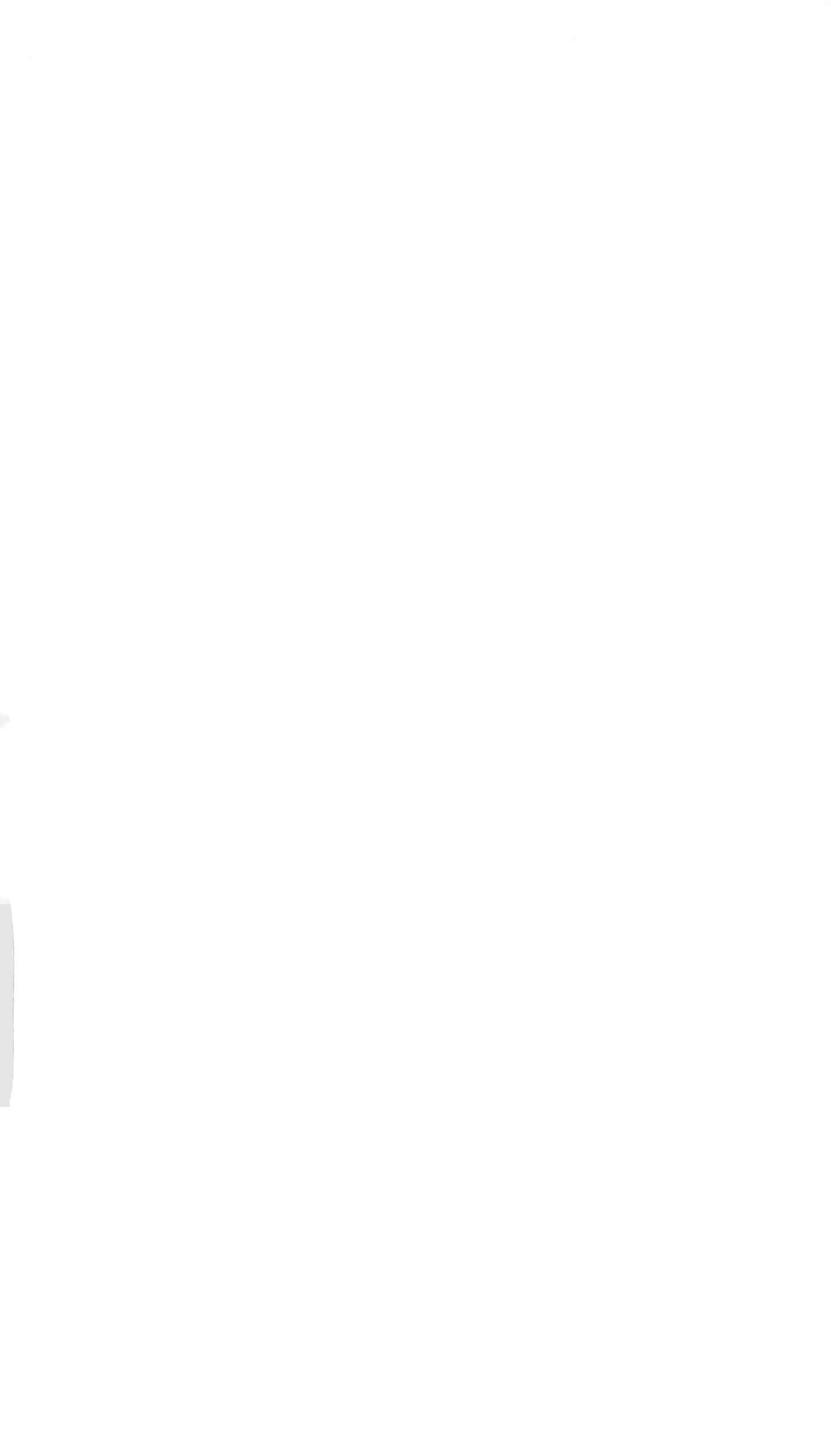

THE PUNITIVE CITY

PRIVATIZED POLICING AND PROTECTION IN NEOLIBERAL MEXICO

MARKUS-MICHAEL MÜLLER

ZED

Zed Books

LONDON

The Punitive City: Privatized Policing and Protection in Neoliberal Mexico was first published in 2016 by Zed Books Ltd, The Foundry, 17 Oval Way, London SE11 5RR, UK.

www.zedbooks.net

Typeset in Sabon by seagulls.net
Index: ed.emery@thefreeuniversity.net
Cover design by roguefour.co.uk

A catalogue record for this book is available from the British Library.

ISBN 978-1-78360-697-9 hb
ISBN 978-1-78360-696-2 pb
ISBN 978-1-78360-698-6 pdf
ISBN 978-1-78360-699-3 epub
ISBN 978-1-78360-700-6 mobi

Printed and bound by CPI Group (UK) Ltd, Croydon, CR0 4YY

CONTENTS

ACKNOWLEDGEMENTS

This book is the result of a more than ten-year journey that started with my first trip to Mexico City in the spring of 2006. The journey began with a dissertation project that was written within the context of a larger research project on public security and human rights in so-called developing democracies. The journey has ended, for the time being, with this book, which addresses what can be described as the 'dark side' of these developments. This book would not have been possible without the support, encouragement, criticism and assistance of many people, including friends and family.

My first thanks are to Marianne Braig who, for nearly twenty years, has been a mentor in the most positive meaning of the word. She has been a constant source of intellectual inspiration and support. It would be impossible to list all the people who, over the course of the last ten years, commented, supported and critically discussed my work on urban security in Mexico City with me. Among those whose comments have helped and inspired me are Carlos Alba Vega, Enrique Desmond Arias, Elena Azaola, Anne Becker, José Carlos Aguiar, Paul E. Amar, Bernd Belina, Benedicte Bull, Didier Fassin, Daniel M. Goldstein, Lirio Gutierrez Rivera, Paul Hathazy, Tina Hilgers, Jana Hönke, Kees Koonings, Reinhard Kreissl, Dirk Kruijt, Claudio Lomnitz, Günther Maihold, Matthias Middell, Wil Pansters, Pablo Piccato, Shalini Randeria, Michael Riekenberg, Veronica Schild, Stefanie Kron, Stephanie Schütze, Jefrey Rubin, Ruth Stanley, Mark Ungar, Loïc Wacquant and Martha Zapata Galindo.

I would also like to thank the academic and administrative staff, past and present, of the ZI Lateinamerika Institut, Freie Universität Berlin, the Collaborative Research Center (SFB) 700 'Governance in Areas of Limited Statehood', Freie Universität Berlin, as well as my former colleagues at the Center for Area Studies, Universität Leipzig, for the inspiring and productive work environments that allowed me to develop most of the ideas presented in this book. At the SFB 700, I also want to thank Eric Stollenwerk and Anne Hehn, for their critical support with bureaucratic and administrative issues.

I am also thankful for the research assistance provided by Frank Müller, Peter Finkenbusch, Birte Keller and, particularly, Carmen Altmeyer, who provided me with invaluable assistance in preparing the final manuscript. I am grateful for the excellent research assistance, including conducting interviews with local residents, provided by Nils Brock and Carlos Alberto Zamudio in Mexico City.

The research for this book was made possible by funding provided by the Deutsche Forschungsgemeinschaft (DFG), the German Federal Ministry of Education (BMBF), as well as the initial financial support, in the form of a PhD research grant (NaFöG), from the Senate of Berlin.

Several of the chapters that follow draw on material that has been published elsewhere. Parts of Chapter 1 draw upon a paper presented at the XXXI International Congress of the Latin American Studies Association, Washington DC, 29 May to 1 June 2013, published in an earlier form as 'Penal Statecraft in the Latin American City: Assessing Mexico City's Punitive Urban Democracy' in *Social and Legal Studies*, 22(4) (2013), 441–463. Sections of Chapter 1 also draw upon an article published as 'The Securitization of Urban Space and the "Rescue" of Downtown Mexico City: Vision and Practice', in *Latin American Perspectives*, 40(2), 77–94. Parts of Chapter 2 appeared as 'Transformaciones del clientelismo: Democratización, (in)seguridad y políticas urbanas en el Distrito Federal', in *Foro Internacional*, 52(4) (2012), 836–863, 'Addressing an Ambivalent Relationship: Policing and the Urban Poor in Mexico City', *Journal of Latin American Studies*, 44(2) (2012), 319–345, and '"Public" Security and Patron-Client Exchanges in Latin America', in *Government & Opposition*, 48(4) (2012), 548–569. The first part of Chapter 3 draws on an article published as 'The Securitization of Urban Space and the "Rescue" of Downtown Mexico City: Vision and Practice', in *Latin American Perspectives*, 40(2), 77–94. The second part of this chapter draws on material that was presented at the 113th Annual

Meeting of the American Anthropological Association, Washington DC, 3–7 December 2014 and lectures given at the Institut for Engelsk, Germansk og Romansk, University of Copenhagen, 17 November 2014 and the Norwegian Institute of International Affairs, 26 August 2014. Chapter 4 draws upon a paper that was presented at the 54th International Congress of Americanists, Vienna, 15–20 July 2012 and published as 'De-Monopolizing the Bureaucratic Field: International-ization Strategies and the Transnationalization of Security Governance in Mexico City', in *Alternatives: Global, Local, Political*, 39(1) (2014), 37–54 and 'The Struggle over Human Rights in Mexico', published in Klaus Hoffmann-Holland (ed.), *Ethics and Human Rights in a Global-ized World*, Tübingen: Mohr-Siebeck (2009), 43–62. Some parts of Chapter 5 draw on material that was presented at the conference 'Crime, Insecurity, Fear in Mexico', Columbia University, New York, 13–14 November 2009 and published as 'Addressing an Ambivalent Relationship: Policing and the Urban Poor in Mexico City', *Journal of Latin American Studies*, 44(2) (2012), 319–345. The chapter also draws upon a paper presented at the XXXIII International Congress of the Latin American Studies Association, Puerto Rico, 27–30 May 2015. I am thankful to the publishers for granting me permission to include this material in this book.

Finally, I want to thank Kika Sroka-Miller, my editor at Zed Books, for her interest in my research and her encouraging professionalism that substantially shaped the final version of this book and made the whole process a very pleasant experience.

Louise Wiuff Moe knows that this book would not have seen the light of day without her loving personal support and sharp intellec-tual criticism. Engaging with my writing through the lens of her own research on Somalia in many ways helped me to see Mexican realities differently and to strengthen several of the book's main arguments. The book was written while she was pregnant with our daughter Mathilde and finalizing the manuscript coincided with Mathilde's birth. The book is dedicated to Louise and Mathilde, for all the love, joy and inspiration the two of you bring into my life every single day.

ABBREVIATIONS

CCE	Empresarial Coordination Council (Consejo Coordinador Empresarial)
CCTV	closed-circuit television
CDHDF	Human Rights Commission of the Federal District (Comisión de Derechos Humanos del Distrito Federal)
CESPEDES	Center for Private Sector Studies for Sustainable Development (Centro de Estudios del Sector Privado para el Desarrollo Sustentable)
FDN	National Democratic Front (Frente Democrático Nacional)
FPFVI	Independent Popular Front Francisco Villa (Frente Popular Francisco Villa Independiente)
INEGI	National Institute of Statistics and Geography (Instituto Nacional de Estadística, Geografía, e Informáticas)
INACIPE	National Institute for Penal Sciences (Instituto Nacional de Ciencias Penales)
INSYDE	Institute for Democracy and Security (Instituto para la Seguridad y la Democracia A.C.)
LED	Extinction of Property Law of the Federal District (Ley de Extinción del Dominio para el Distrito Federal)
GDF	Government of the Federal District (Gobierno del Distrito Federal)
LCC	Civic Culture Law of the Federal District (Ley de Cultura Cívica del Distrito Federal)

NAFTA	North American Free Trade Agreement
NGO	non-governmental organization
PAN	National Action Party (Partido Acción Nacional)
PRD	Democratic Revolutionary Party (Partido de la Revolución Democrática)
PRI	Institutional Revolutionary Party (Partido Revolucionario Institucional)
SSPDF	Secretariat of Public Security of the Federal District (Secretaría de Seguridad Pública del Distrito Federal)
UPC	Citizen Protection Unit (Unidad de Protección Ciudadana)

INTRODUCTION

Let's begin this book with the narration of a short scene:

A group of poor adolescents has access, by accident, to the walled space of a gated community. They make use of this opportunity and step inside. They enter a house, look around and steal a few things. They are detected. A resident, a private security guard and two of the intruders die in a shootout. One of the adolescents manages to escape. Due to a video surveillance system, the residents of the gated community know that at least one of the boys is still inside. A meeting is held and the residents decide to solve the problem without the help of the police, as they fear that official involvement would strip them of their legal right to self-administration. They form armed patrols and search for the boy. The police arrive. After the residents agree to contribute a monetary donation to the 'improvement' of the police, they receive a guarantee from the commanding officer that nobody will interfere with their actions. The boy manages to hide for a couple of days with the help of a local teenager but is then discovered. After an unsuccessful attempt to escape, a mob of local residents beats him to death. His body is dumped in the rubbish; the teenager from the gated community finds his dead body and takes him to a cemetery to receive an informal burial – at least.

The setting for this story is Mexico City. It is a fictitious story told in the fascinating movie *La Zona* (2007), directed by Rodrigo Plá. This movie, like many other contemporary Mexican cultural offerings, provides an insight into the cultural representation and imagination of one of the most pressing problems in contemporary Mexico – the question of crime and insecurity. But the scene described above is not just about crime and insecurity. Rather, it offers a cultural representation of the complex and contradictory entanglements linking crime, insecurity and the privatization of security and punishment – mediated by informal practices – in contemporary Mexico City, a relationship whose social and political (re-)making through various 'securitization' processes transforms Mexico City into a *punitive city*. The analysis of this transformation process lies at the centre of this book.

Latin America's new urban punitiveness

The term 'punitive city' is borrowed from criminologist Stanley Cohen. In an article published in 1979 Cohen used the metaphor of the punitive city to reflect on changes in forms of social control and punishment. The overall trend he saw unfolding at that time was a 'dispersal of social control'. For Cohen, one important indicator of this dispersion of social control was a growing tendency toward its privatization and a more general 'merging of the obviously public and formal apparatus of control with the private and less formal' (Cohen 1979: 353). The implications of these developments, according to Cohen, were the following: '[O]n the one hand, the repressive, interventionist reach of the state should be blunted, on the other, the "community" should become more involved in the day to day business of prevention and control' (ibid.). Published only six years after Pinochet's coup against the democratically-elected social democratic government of Salvador Allende in Chile on 11 September 1973, which triggered 'the first great experiment with neoliberal state formation' (Harvey 2006: 12), Cohen's article captured some of the first consequences related to the travelling and execution of the test results of the 'Chilean experiment' (on this issue, see Barder 2013) within the penal realm of the United States and the United Kingdom.

The emerging patterns and practices Cohen analysed in his article were part and parcel of a more general transformation that, during the next two decades, transformed neoliberal state formation into what Loïc Wacquant (2009a) describes as *penal state* formation. Contrary to dominant myths about the general downsizing of the state under neoliberalism, Wacquant identifies a broader re-making of the state that substantially enhances the size and weight of its penal apparatus, that is, the courts, police and prison systems. In a longer passage worth quoting, Wacquant argues:

> The regulation of the working classes through what Pierre Bourdieu calls 'the Left Hand' of the state, that which protects and expands life chances, represented by labor law, education, health, social assistance, and public housing is supplanted (in the United States) or supplemented (in the European Union) by regulation through its 'Right Hand,' that of the police, justice, correctional administration, increasingly active and intrusive in the subaltern zones of social and urban space. [...] The renewed utility of the penal apparatus in the post-Keynesian era of insecure employment is threefold: (1) it works to bend the fractions of the working class recalcitrant to the discipline of the new fragmented service wage-labor by increasing the cost of strategies of exit into the informal economy of the street; (2) it neutralizes and warehouses its most disruptive elements, or those rendered wholly superfluous by the recomposition of the demand for labor; and (3) it reaffirms the authority of the state in daily life within the restricted domain henceforth assigned to it. (Wacquant 2009a: 6–7)

During the last two decades, these processes travelled back to Latin America. As a result, they have contributed to a hitherto unparalleled increase in the region's inmate population that, in relative and absolute terms, exceeds historical levels of incarceration (Hathazy and Müller 2016), and to a broader punitive turn in local politics (Goldstein 2012; Gutiérrez Rivera 2013; Hathazy 2013; Hathazy and Müller 2016; Iturralde 2010; Müller 2016a, 2015, 2012a, 2012b; Wacquant 2008a).

As Latin America 'is the most highly urbanized region in the global South', with nearly 80 per cent of the region's population living in cities (Perlman 2010: 46), these processes are, therefore, mostly visible in the region's urban areas. In this regard, throughout the region, the 'urbanization of neoliberalism' (Brenner and Theodore 2002) of the last three decades was accompanied by an increasingly punitive turn in urban governance rationales that, following Neil Smith, can be classified as a form of 'urban revanchism' (Smith 1996). In drawing a parallel between the revanchist political movement – which formed in the last decades of the nineteenth century in France, as a reaction against the liberalism of the Second Republic, the defeat of France in the Franco-German war and the experience of the Paris Commune – and more contemporary political attitudes among neoliberal political and economic elites, Smith argues that, like their right-wing nineteenth-century counterparts in their efforts to organize a movement of revenge and reaction against the unruly working class and the discredited royalty, since the 1990s neoliberal urban governance has increasingly taken the form of an urban revanchism, directed against imagined urban 'enemies' (Smith 1996: 42). The outcome of these revanchist policies is a form of 'reaction and vengeance' directed against 'people which could be perceived as if they had "stolen" the city from its legitimate proprietors (the middle class and investors)' (Smith 2005: 71).

Within the context of the above-mentioned travelling back of neoliberal (penal) state formation experiments to Latin America, 'revanchist urbanism' was heading south (Swanson 2007). It spread throughout the region, leading to what John Gledhill recently termed 'the new war on the poor' in Latin America (Gledhill 2015). The main victims of this war, Gledhill demonstrates, are communities that are '"inconvenient" in a contemporary capitalist context for a number of reasons […] that boil down to the principle that capital accumulation can be enhanced through the removal of barriers to its penetration of the spaces that these inconvenient populations occupy, and barriers to its ability to extract the maximum profit from selling goods and services within them' (ibid.: 18).

Securitizing democracies

Concurring with Gledhill's analysis, this book argues that securitization processes are central elements of this development. The term 'securitization' was coined by international relations scholars of the Copenhagen School (e.g., Buzan et al. 1998; Buzan and Hansen 2009; Wæver 1995). The term reflects a constructivist understanding of security. Security, as a discursive reference point, is not something that simply exists 'out there'. Rather, security issues and risks are the product of political construction processes through political speech acts. As security is a relational concept, always referring to and dependent upon the construction of its 'other', securitization practices are always accompanied by processes of '(in)securitization'. The latter term refers to 'successful political speech act(s) transforming the decision making process and generating a politics of exception, often favoring coercive options' (Bigo and Tsoukala 2008: 5; see also Müller 2016a). When a specific issue becomes securitized, 'it passes on from the realm of ordinary politicized questions, becoming an issue that threatens the very survival of states and their citizens, defined not as individuals but as the collective object "society"' (Gledhill 2015: 19).

In places like Mexico, but also in many other countries in contemporary Latin America, the end of authoritarian rule and military dictatorships led to the emergence of neoliberal 'securitized democracies' (Pearce 2010). The latter can be seen as a direct response to the 'democratization of violence' (Koonings and Kruijt 1999: 15) that accompanied the region's democratic transition processes, leading to the consolidation of 'violent democracies' (Arias and Goldstein 2010a). In this regard, as Koonings and Kruijt have argued, while formerly 'the use of violence was restricted to certain sectors: the aristocracy, the elite, the army', in post-transition Latin America the 'proliferation of violence, even in its more anomic forms, has reached the stage of mass production and mass consumption' (Koonings and Kruijt 1999: 15). With the related emergence of what has been termed 'new violence' – a violence that stands in contrast to the 'old', predominantly political violence, which defined the decades of authoritarian rule – the use of violence is 'not primarily [...] an ideological grounded means to secure formal political or state power but rather [...] a flexible source to attain other goals, especially economic gains or social status' (Koonings 2012: 255–256). However, as Koonings and Kruijt recently argued, what was seen as 'new' in the mid-1990s is today's new normal in Latin America (Koonings and Kruijt 2015a: 5).

The most tragic evidence of this development is probably the fact that Latin America has become one of the world's most violent regions, and the world's 'only region with rising homicide rates between 2000 and 2010' (ibid.: 4). According to the Homicide Monitor of the Brazilian think tank Igarapé Institute, the most comprehensive publicly available dataset on homicides, 33 per cent of all reported homicides worldwide occur in Latin America and the Caribbean, a region that is home to only 8 per cent of the world's population. Consequently, the region is home to '14 of the 20 most dangerous countries in the world'. In addition, more than '130 large Latin American and Caribbean cities register very high homicide rates (i.e. higher than 25 per 100,000)'.* Latin America's new violent normality, as reflected in these high homicide numbers, however, is inseparable from persistent patterns of socio-economic inequality and exclusion that deepened under neoliberalism, as well as the related 'expansion of informal domains of livelihood and sociability as well as the fragility of the state and the public domain, especially with respect to the rule of law and citizens' security' (Koonings 2012: 255).

In the Latin American democratic context, in which electoral outcomes now determine the survival of politicians (and bureaucrats), neoliberalism, under the banner of austerity politics, confronts many governments with structural constraints regarding the provision of jobs and public services. And as voters are increasingly concerned about a real as well as perceived deterioration of their personal security and safety, governments and politicians throughout the region securitized the issue of crime in order to mobilize political support and secure electoral gains in a democratic context. Accordingly, the crime problem has become a political opportunity for winning elections as well as for promoting political and bureaucratic careers. In the words of Paul Chevigny:

---

* https://igarape.org.br/en/homicide-monitor/

The pressures to draw upon the fear of crime for political advantage are enormous. Because the governments adhere to neo-liberal policies, and usually cannot promise a large number of jobs or other relief measures to their constituents, politicians are confronted with constant social protest, to which they must make some reply, even if they cannot promise relief. [...] When the rise of crime is of great concern to voters, it would seem all but irresistible for politicians to turn the voters' attention to personal security. (Chevigny 2003: 83)

Most countries in the region, as evidenced by the growing expansion of the Latin American inmate population, have not resisted these pressures. Rather, most governments – national as well as subnational and irrespective of their political orientations (Hathazy and Müller 2016) – have embraced the politicization of crime in order to keep themselves in power by waging veritable securitization campaigns that have transformed the region's newly emerging democracies into securitized democracies. The securitization processes at the heart of these developments continuously produce security discourses that divide the social space into two antagonizing camps, that of 'citizens' on the one hand and that of 'anticitizens of a neoliberal social order' (Thomas et al. 2011: 12) on the other. These discourses, and resulting policies, produce populations that are at the same time 'disposable' (Denyer Willis 2015) and 'outlawed' (Goldstein 2012). With the latter term, Goldstein, in his ethnography of the lived experiences of (in)security of those at urban society's margins in Cochabamba, Bolivia, refers to people that 'live outside the protection of state law, yet they are multiply subjected to its constraints; they must do without the law's benefits, but they are criminalized as *illegal occupants of urban space*' (Goldstein 2012: 3, emphasis added). In fact, nowhere are these processes of punitive outlawing and the production of disposability more visible than in the highly unequal urban spaces of the region. Throughout the last two decades, most Latin American cities have witnessed a veritable 'securitization of urban space', defined as 'the hegemony of security and (dis)order concerns regarding the "proper" use, design, and (re)ordering of urban space' (Becker and Müller 2013: 79). It is this securitization of urban space that transforms the region's cities into *punitive cities*, which have become the main battlefields of the new war on the poor waged in contemporary Latin America.*

While top-down political interests in 'making crime pay' (Beckett 1999) – and the resulting policies of penal institution building as well as the deployment of repressive 'zero tolerance' (Swanson 2013) and even counterinsurgency approaches (Hochmüller and Müller 2016; Müller 2016b; Moe and Müller 2015) – within the new war on the poor contributed substantially to the punitive turn in contemporary Latin American politics, the growing punitiveness throughout the region cannot be reduced to these top-down processes. Rather, the punitive turn in contemporary Latin American politics must be understood as an 'ambivalent convergence of top-down and bottom-up punitivism' (Hathazy and Müller 2016: 128). Teresa Caldeira's work on urban Brazil, for instance, has shown that notwithstanding 'many problems with the formal justice system, many poor urban residents nevertheless advocate for a stronger and more aggressive police presence in their neighbourhoods, contending that crime would be reduced and security enhanced were the authorities to take a heavy-handed approach (la mano dura) to crime in the streets' (Caldeira 2006: 21). Moreover, as Graham Denyer Willis' work indicates, such top-down processes are accompanied by and embedded in a bottom-up 'proliferation of self-help security in many cities of the Global South, but acutely in Latin America' (Denyer Willis 2015: 8). A veritable expansion of 'private vigilantism' (Koonings and Kruijt 2007: 15) can be seen throughout the region, where, partly in response to the inefficiency of the formal security and justice institutions, citizens are taking security and justice into their own hands. The manifestations of this development are manifold. They include 'private police, privately paid street guardians in the middle-class and even the working-class metropolitan districts, private citizens' *serengazos* (nightwatch committees or private protection squads), special forces in the financial sector recruited from former police forces and the army, extra-legal task forces, paramilitary commandos, death

---

* For a global perspective on urban securitization processes, see Lippert and Walby (2013).

squads, and so on' (ibid.). These bottom-up 'forms of decentralized security' are complicit in the top-down punitive turn as they 'complement, aggravate, consolidate, and criminalize deeply historical modes of urban exclusion along known racial, spatial, and class lines' (Denyer Willis 2015: 8).

Mexico City as a 'workshop' of punitive urban democratization

This book assesses these processes, their causes and punitive consequences from the vantage point of Mexico City. Debates on Mexico's security problems are usually centred on the escalating drug violence that accompanied the 'war against drugs' declared by Mexican president Felipe Calderón Hinojosa (2006–2012) from the National Action Party (PAN) (e.g., Kenny and Serrano 2012; Morton 2012; Watt and Zepeda 2012). In bypassing the dominant drug war narrative, and by restoring politics to the centre of analysis, this book offers an in-depth assessment of the more mundane yet even more pervasive punitive turn in urban Mexico that cannot be reduced to, nor explained with, the Mexican drug war. In fact, 'Mexico City seems to be an enclave within a country that, in a certain sense, is torn apart by drug-related armed confrontations' (Koonings and Kruijt 2015a: 24). In analysing the transformation of Mexico City into a punitive city, a city in which punitive practices have dispersed and top-down and bottom-up penalizing practices have converged in ambivalent and contingent ways that deepen the overall punitive re-making of urban governance, the book offers a case study of the 'ordinary' punitive turn in one of the region's most important cities. It provides important insights for understanding similar processes at work in other Latin American cities. The main argument of this book is that the transformation of Mexico City into a punitive city is inseparable from the urbanization of neoliberalism, the repercussions of the local democratization process and the political top-down and bottom-up (re-) workings of, and responses to, urban insecurity.

Mexico City provides a uniquely promising context for assessing the role of politics in the making of the punitive city. First of all, crime and insecurity are nothing new for the city and its 8.9 million residents (INEGI 2011: 8).* Modern Mexico City, in the words of historian Pablo Piccato, has always been a 'city of suspects' in which for 'the majority of the city's inhabitants, crime was an integral part of everyday life' (Piccato 2001: 3). The transformation of the city of suspects into a punitive city, thus, is not a natural response to crime and insecurity. This book demonstrates that the emergence of the punitive city cannot be understood without taking into consideration the more recent politicization of (in)security through various securitization discourses, which are directly related to the arrival of neoliberal urban governing rationalities, on the one hand, and the democratization of local politics, on the other.

By relating the punitive turn in local politics to the democratization of local governance, the book challenges normative and theoretical assumptions of scholars from what Arias and Goldstein (2010b: 10) have termed the 'democratization school'. This school of thought that dominates contemporary research on Latin American politics, promotes a minimalist conception of democracy as 'polyarchy', assuming that a democracy exists wherever formal institutions are in place and social, political and legal rights essential for these institutions to operate are granted to the local population. However, as evidenced by Arias and Goldstein, the

> exclusive focus on elections, institutions and rights [...] avoids the messy realities of actually existing political systems as they are found in Latin America (and elsewhere) today. Particularly problematic to these models is the existence of widespread violence, criminality, and insecurity in nations whose political systems might otherwise be characterized as democratic if not polyarchic. (ibid.)

In fact, in terms of the coexistence of violence, insecurity and formal democracy, Mexico City realities, as well as those in many other

---

* Mexico City, in this book, refers to the Federal District, Mexico's capital city. The Federal District is part of the Zona metropolitana del Valle de México, comprising the Federal District, as well as fifty-nine municipalities of the neighbouring State of Mexico and one municipality of the State of Hidalgo. The Metropolitan Area has a population of about 18.5 million (INEGI 2004: 46) and is one of the world's largest urban agglomerations.

Latin American cities, are '[i]ncongruent with democratic theory and decades of supposed transition' (Denyer Willis 2015: 11). This is the case because the underlying conceptual framework of the democratization school 'privileges changing institutional and noncoercive forms and modalities, thereby (unintentionally) obscuring the harsh realities of a darker Mexico of bullets and blood, one that seems to exist (and to have existed) at a distance, albeit functional, from the institutional realities of ballots and legal battles' (Pansters 2012a: 8). In general, democratization scholars tend to take the 'domestic democratic peace' (Davenport 2007a) argument for granted. That is, they assume 'that democratic political institutions and activities decrease state repressive behavior' (Davenport 2007b: 11). Such reasoning, however, ignores that, irrespective of the type of the political regime (democratic or authoritarian), from an urban perspective 'the state's reliance on police has long been a critical armament in a larger arsenal of coercive tactics employed by the state to establish urban social and spatial order' (Davis 2015: 76).

By analysing how and why security issues become politicized in a democratic context – from the top down and bottom-up and how this leads to repressive policing and criminalizing law-making – this book explains the political reasoning of democratic actors acting in a neoliberal environment in privileging security over other policy concerns in their efforts of reordering cities in social and spatial terms. The book shows how this leads to an overemphasis in local urban governance on (in)security and punishment instead of freedom and liberty – a decision that is mostly felt by those at urban society's margins.

An analysis of the punitive turn in Mexico City, however, not only offers a critical assessment of the 'domestic democratic peace' argument under neoliberalism, it also sheds light on the, at first sight, counterintuitive decision of popular forces coming into office to criminalize and punish exactly those segments of the local population that represent their most important electoral constituency. Taking an in-depth look at the policies implemented by the democratic governments of the leftist Democratic Revolutionary Party (PRD), which has governed Mexico City since the re-introduction of elections for the city mayor in 1997, offers important insights into similar developments observable throughout other Latin American countries of the region's turn to the left, or the so-called 'pink tide' (Burbach et al. 2013; Chodor 2015; Weyland 2010). While leftist governments that came to power in the 2000s in many of the region's countries, including Argentina, Brazil, Bolivia, Chile, Ecuador and Venezuela, implemented redistributive politics and social/welfare programmes that contributed substantially to the fact that Latin America – which is still among the most unequal world regions in terms of income distribution – recently 'experienced some of the largest reductions in poverty levels' worldwide' (Koonings and Kruijt 2015a: 8), most leftist governments also implemented penalizing politics that made them join the new war on the poor. The resulting simultaneous expansion of welfare and punitive politics in contemporary Latin America is one of the defining features of Latin American penal state formation (Müller 2012a; Schild 2015), indicating, as argued above, that punitive politics are not the monopoly of right-wing governments. On the contrary, the punitive turn can also be observed in countries often presented as textbook examples of emancipatory and alternative politics, such as Brazil, Venezuela, Bolivia or Ecuador, all of which demonstrate rising inmate populations – mostly composed of urban marginals – that are often accompanied by repressive law enforcement approaches (Amar 2013; Antillano et al. 2016; Garces 2014; Goldstein 2012; Silvestre 2016; Swanson 2010). In explaining how and why a democratically elected leftist party in Mexico City chose to pursue a punitive urban governing agenda, the book investigates and highlights the structural challenges confronted by popular forces coming to political power in contemporary neoliberal urban Latin America as well as the ambivalent policy outcomes resulting from these challenges.

The chapters that follow will zoom in on key sites, actors, processes and instances of this punitive transformation process that serve as privileged analytical vantage points for uncovering the complex and contradictory entanglements that contribute to the making of the punitive city. The analysis draws upon interviews conducted in Mexico City between 2006 and 2011, field notes, local newspapers, official government documents as well as reports by non-governmental organizations (NGOs). My overall interest and aim is not so much to come up with an all-encompassing causal story or theoretical account for the transformation of Mexico City into a punitive city. Rather, I demonstrate that the concept of the punitive city should be seen as a heuristic lens for assessing these often neglected, and for some even unexpected, aspects of urban governance in contemporary Mexico City (and elsewhere in Latin America). To this end, the term punitive city can be considered as something like a 'loose-knit conceptual orientation' (see Collier and Ong 2005: 5–6) that serves to integrate the chapters that follow into a coherent analytical narrative for assessing the complex, ambivalent, and often contradictory processes and actors involved in the making of the punitive city. The story that follows is, in this respect, biased. It focuses on aspects that are key drivers behind the punitive turn in local governance while neglecting other aspects of local urban governance. However, as the city's punitive turn has not received sufficient attention in the debates on security in contemporary Mexico, this bias, in my view, not only seems to be justified but is, indeed, necessary. It sensitizes readers to the penalizing consequences of the securitization of academic and policy debates on democratic governance in contemporary urban Latin America and hopefully opens up future debates that avoid the securitizing consequences and frameworks that so far, even if unintentionally, have contributed to the perpetuation of social exclusion, marginalization and criminalization of those at urban society's margins in the name of security.

Organization of the book

Chapter 1 provides the macro-structural context for the analysis of the punitive turn in Mexico City politics. It demonstrates how and why the intersection of the urbanization of neoliberalism, the democratization of local politics and the rise of the PRD during the local democratization process contributed to a growing penalization of urban marginality, and the related transformation of Mexico City into a punitive city. The latter is characterized by the punitive governing of urban marginality that increasingly excludes, through criminalization and penalization, the most marginalized segments of the urban population, in particular those labouring in the city's expanding informal – and criminalized – economy, whose lives the local democratization process was expected to improve.

Chapter 2 builds on these findings and assesses their implications within the realm of informal politics by analysing the resilience of political clientelism in the punitive city. As the democratization of Mexico City politics was accompanied by and embedded in a growing deterioration of the local security situation, in a mutually reinforcing process bottom-up demands for protection led to the discovery of the political gains local politicians and political brokers could gain from offering informal protection in exchange for political support. The overall result of this has been the diversification of the spectrum of clientelist 'services', as well as the expansion of clientelism into the realm of security governance and the more punitive transformation of urban politics.

By turning to the unfolding of neoliberal urban renewal processes in the Merced and Tepito neighbourhoods, Chapter 3 offers a bottom-up perspective on the place specificity of urban revanchism in the punitive city. It stresses the mediation of larger macro-structural processes of neoliberal place-making by informal practices and multiple forms of resistance as well as contestation that are illustrative of the ongoing difficulties and the complex nature of the expansion of neoliberal urban renewal projects, and the corresponding securitization of urban space in neighbourhoods such as the Merced or Tepito. Here local residents, as well as illegal(ized) informal economic and political actors, engage in multiple forms of resistance to contest and negotiate the neoliberal 'upgrading' of their neighbourhoods and the related processes of securitization and penalization.

In analysing the emergence of a community of NGOs whose work focuses on security issues, Chapter 4 demonstrates how the import of security-related knowledge, expertise and international best practice, far from improving the local security situation, actually reinforces the penalizing tendencies of urban governance in contemporary Mexico City. In this regard, the chapter highlights the implicit complicity of securitizing civic activism in the making of the punitive city. The chapter stresses the contribution such NGOs make to the punitive turn in local politics by facilitating the import of punitive policing models, such as zero tolerance policing. Moreover, the chapter demonstrates how this form of security expertise has become a veritable business model that enhances the power of technocratic NGOs that present themselves as impartial security experts at the expense of more politically oriented civic organizations.

The analysis of multiple bottom-up efforts by Mexico City residents to search for more protection in an insecure urban environment sits at the centre of Chapter 5. It will be demonstrated that such bottom-up responses to insecurity, ranging from different forms of self-policing and community justice to the informal as well as formal commodification of protection, reinforce those top-down punitive efforts that, during the last decade, converted Mexico City into a punitive city. Be it through the construction of us vs. them identities that reproduce penal populism's antagonizing logics of a 'threatened' us and a criminal 'other' at the neighbourhood level, the contracting of security guards, coercive bribery and the related appropriation of police forces for private (punitive) purposes, or the taking of the law literally into one's own hands, Mexico City residents, in their efforts to deal with neoliberal violence, are active agents in the punitive transformation of the city.

The concluding chapter summarizes the main findings of the book. In light of this, the conclusion ends with a call for a desecuritization of political and academic discourse, as well as for an alternative research agenda that, by embedding the question of (in)security within a broader interdisciplinary political-economy analytical framework, might be able to identify alternative responses towards urban violence that could possibly challenge the ongoing criminalization of urban marginality throughout the region.

CHAPTER 1

The making of the punitive city

In June 2004, several hundred thousand Mexico City residents mobilized by civil society organizations like *México Unido Contra la Delincuencia* (Mexico United Against Delinquency), the country's most influential anti-crime NGOs, rallied to the streets of the nation's capital in order to protest against the inefficiency of the Mexican authorities in their efforts to confront the crime wave haunting the city, and the country in general, as well as the leniency of existing penal laws. In this regard, the protest was accompanied by widespread demands for retributive punishment and 'tough on crime' policies, including calls for indefinite prison terms and the death penalty for kidnappers and murderers (*La Jornada* 2004a, 2004b). Nearly three years later, in spring 2007, car drivers and pedestrians strolling down one of Mexico City's most trafficked streets, Insurgentes Avenue, were confronted with a huge billboard on top of a multi-storey building. The billboard, placed there by a private initiative, offered a reward of 250,000 Mexican Pesos (then about US$ 23,000) for the capture of a presumed kidnapper and murderer – a capture that was called a 'community service'. A year later, Mexico's Green Ecological Party distributed leaflets among urban households in Mexico City. The leaflet contained two photo stories. One story was about María, whose daughter had been kidnapped and who was threatened by Moncho, a prisoner, to pay the full ransom, otherwise her daughter would have to suffer the consequences. María, the story tells us, despite financial support from her mother, was unable to pay the complete ransom and she never heard from her daughter again. The other story is about Juan, presented as a 'repeat offender'. He was waiting at a street corner for his next victim. When a young boy and girl got off a bus, Juan tried to assault them, but the young man attempted to defend himself. A dramatic series of photos show how Juan stabbed the young man, who died in the arms of his girlfriend. Below the photos, and next to the ecological party's symbol, the leaflet reads: 'Death penalty for kidnappers and murderers. Let's make it real and live in peace.'

These episodes are snapshots of a larger punitive turn in urban politics that accompanied the democratization of the Mexican political system throughout the last two decades and which transformed Mexico City into a punitive city. This development, as this book demonstrates, is not primarily, nor exclusively, related to a real increase in urban crime and insecurity. Rather, it is inseparable from the imposition of a neoliberal vision of economic, social and political order, as well as a new regime of governing urban marginality that is driven by securitization processes that translate into the criminalization and penalization of those at urban society's margins (Wacquant 2009a). As this process is simultaneously overdetermined by the democratization of local politics, the punitive turn in Mexico City converts the city into a veritable punitive urban democracy. A democracy in which, notwithstanding the formal legal empowerment and growing political inclusion of urban residents, a growing number of the city's residents, in particular those at the urban margins, are confronted with a reverse process of punitive exclusion.

This chapter will outline the basic features of this process and highlight the ambivalent, and at first sight, contradictory relationship between the democratization of local politics and the growing penalization of urban marginality. In stressing how the intersection of these processes, and their embeddedness within the rolling-out of neoliberalism, contributed to the transformation of Mexico City into a punitive city, this chapter provides the general context for the subsequent parts of this book by indicating how the urbanization of neoliberalism in Mexico City and its intersection with idiosyncratic features of the local political situation led to the punitive turn in Mexico's capital city.

The punitive logic of urban neoliberalism in Mexico City

Like in most other Latin American countries during the last twenty years or so, Mexico's political economy shifted from a semi-peripheral version of Fordism – grounded in import-substituting industrialization and politically regulated by the corporatist state structures that defined the country's authoritarian regime under the seventy-one years (1929–2000) of uninterrupted one-party rule by the Institutional Revolutionary Party (PRI) – towards a neoliberal free-market economy under the auspices of an 'international competition state' that promotes 'pro-competition and pro-market policy' (Soederberg 2010: 77; see also Heigl 2011). Mexico City was severely affected by these macro-economical transformations. Not only did these processes contribute to a breakdown of the local manufacturing sector that had been central to the city's economy throughout most of the twentieth century, Mexico City also lost its national importance as the centre of economic decision making. Between 1982 and 1989, for instance, the number of Mexican top 500 companies located in the city declined from 287 to 145 (Parnreiter 2002). This development was accompanied by the broader decline of formal economic activities, 'the spread of micro businesses and the unprecedented expansion of the informal sector' (Vargas Hernández and Reza Noruzi 2011: 89). While the actual size of the city's informal economy is difficult to assess, it is widely assumed that around 50 per cent of all jobs in the city are in the informal sector (ILO 2014: 5), which is about 10 per cent below the national average of around 60 per cent (ibid.; OECD 2013: 52). In Mexico City, the informal economy is highly concentrated in the area of Mexico City's historic centre (Castillo Olea 2006: 1). Although the city's economy recovered throughout the second half of the 1990s, this process was obtained at the further expense of formal employment and social standards and accompanied by deteriorating/stagnating income levels. In turn, this left ever larger segments of the urban workforce few options for economic survival other than joining the informal economy, which became the fastest growing segment of the urban labour market (Parnreiter 2002: 148–154).

It is this growing informalization of the city's economy that triggered a punitive response from the local authorities. In order to understand this outcome, one has to take a closer look at the basis of the recovery of the city's economy. The latter was, more than anything else, the result of 'a deep tertiarization process, which for the urban region [of Mexico City] meant the shift from a national industrial metropolis to a transnational node for financial flows and specialized consumption' (Kanai and Ortega Alcazár 2009: 487). These processes continued well into the new millennium. In 2004, 73 per cent of all foreign companies operating in Mexico had their headquarters in Mexico City and the city's producer service sector, notably services related to finance, insurance and business management, generated 76.5 per cent of the *national* added value. More striking than this is the fact that around 55 per cent of the overall national added value were generated in only three, centrally located boroughs, or *delegaciones* (Cuauhtémoc, Miguel Hidalgo and Benito Juárez) (Parnreiter 2011: 7–9). Such indicators clearly demonstrate that Mexico City's economic recovery has been accompanied by the city's rise to the status of a Global City (Parnreiter 2011, 2002; Graizboard et al. 2003). As other Global Cities, Mexico City now functions as a 'command point' for an increasingly globalized world economy; it has become a key location for finance and other specialized producer services that have largely displaced manufacturing as the leading economic sector; it is a production (and innovation) site for these service industries as well as a market for their products (Sassen 1991: 3–4).

This, however, did not happen naturally. Mexico City's rise to the status of a Global City resulted from active policy interventions by the local administrations which, since the 1990s, implemented a neoliberal, entrepreneur-friendly mode of urban governance, which largely centres on a reorientation of the local state's responsibilities, in particular within the field of urban economic development. The local state no longer conceives itself as the director of the local economy but as a *facilitator*, that is, as an agency responsible for the creation of an entrepreneur-friendly fiscal policy, an investment-friendly legal climate and the provision of infrastructure for investment projects, with the goal of attracting new national and international investors (Hofmeister 2003: chapter 4). While some of these processes were well underway since Mexican neoliberalism became definitely 'locked-in' under the 'technocratic revolution' (Centeno 1997) of president

Salinas de Gortari (1988–1994, PRI) and his successor Ernesto López Zedillo (1994–2000, PRI), the democratization of Mexico City politics, culminating in the electoral victory of Cuauthémoc Cárdenas in 1997 from the leftist PRD, did not alter this situation. Even with a leftist party in power – a party whose electoral success largely depended upon the promise of improving social welfare services for the urban poor – the centrality of neoliberal urban economic policies in the guise of an adherence to free market principles, the creation of an investment-friendly environment and the strengthening of Mexico City's interurban competitiveness were firmly established, if not strengthened. Indeed, the PRD's vision of urban governance is firmly committed to the principles of economic 'productivity, rentability and competitiveness' (PGDDF 2000: 105), leading to the implementation of the 'standard' neoliberal urban development strategy of actively promoting 'real estate and finance sectors as the leading forces in urban expansion and local revenue generation' (Angotti 2013a: 63).

In order to make sense of this situation, it must be kept in mind that since the PRD established its power in Mexico City, all local administrations have been confronted with either PRI or PAN presidents at the national level, where, according to Mexico's federal system, many of the city's spending priorities and federal fiscal transfers are determined (frequently on a discretionary basis). These national actors, out of political reasoning, had little interest in improving the local mayor's economic and political performance – and financial resources – as they were fearful that such a success could be converted into political capital (see also Davis and Alvarado 2004: 147–51; Mitchell and Beckett 2008: 93; Müller 2009a). While the democratization of Mexico City enhanced the city's political autonomy, the price that had to be paid for this, however, was that the local administrations became increasingly dependent upon their own revenue-generating capacity; a process that, as argued by Weber in another context, makes cities increasingly dependent upon those economic activities promising the fast generation of such desperately needed revenue, in particular private real-estate markets (Weber 2002: 190). Additionally, and closely related, Mexico City's urban policies, including infrastructure investments for its Global City strategy, are also dependent upon debt and credit and, in this regard, on international (mostly

US-based) rating agencies like Standard & Poor's, Moody's or Fitch, whose ratings for Mexico City are displayed on the website of Mexico City's Secretariat of Finance.* Local bureaucrats and politicians are well aware of the impact of credit ratings for their own careers but also for their political projects and constituencies, and therefore chose to adopt the preferred policies and 'expert knowledge' regarding the essential minimization of risk, 'predicated on a firm belief in the efficiency and necessity of US-style neoliberal market reforms' (Mitchell and Beckett 2008: 92). As a consequence of this

> Leftist mayors like Obrador and his successor, Marcelo Ebrard [both succeeded Cárdenas], find themselves caught between their political promises of local spending for needed social services and the all-important movement of bond values and ratings operating on a transnational scale. Their desperate desire to maintain strong relations with U.S.-dominated [rating] agencies frequently leads to municipal policies at odds with their stated mandates of poverty alleviation, *including new 'security measures' intended to drive drug-smugglers and sidewalk merchants out of particular neighborhoods.* (Mitchell and Beckett 2008: 94, emphasis added)

This need to 'drive drug-smugglers and sidewalk merchants out of particular neighbourhoods', for the sake of good credit ratings and urban competitiveness, is mostly felt within the area of Mexico City's historic centre.† This area became the focus of an urban development strategy that aims at transforming this part of the city into an ideal location for (national and international) economic investments in the areas of real estate development, heritage tourism and cultural consumerism (Davis 2013; Linares 2008: 180; Capron and Monnet 2003). The

---

* www.finanzas.df.gob.mx/inv/

† In 1980 a large territory of the old city centre was declared a protected Monument Zone by presidential decree. In 1987, UNESCO proclaimed said historical centre to be a World Heritage Site. The area, which comprises approximately 3.5 square miles and 7,000 buildings, is divided into two zones: the 1.4 square mile Perimeter A, which contains the majority of the listed monuments and buildings (over 1,600) and roughly encompasses the boundaries of the colonial city, and the approximately 2.1 square mile Perimeter B, which accounts for the territorial extension of the city in the nineteenth century.

core of this strategy lies in the articulation and promotion of 'historical heritage and local traditions alongside modern developments to improve the competitiveness of the megacity in the global economy' (Canclini 2008: 191). While this also included the partial privatization of the city's central square, the Zócalo, where, following a commercial agreement between the local government and powerful economic actors, since 2003 all of the free open-air concerts and cultural events taking place on the Zócalo are 'organized by a private trust representing some of Mexico's largest economic actors' (Kanai and Ortega Alcázar 2009: 488), the core of this urban development strategy is the so-called 'rescue project', the Programa de Rescate, implemented in 2001: 'an entrepreneurial strategy characterized by public-private alliances established for the physical transformation of urban space at the expense of poor sectors of the urban population' (Crossa 2009: 45).

The economic success of the resulting urban development strategy becomes apparent when considering that in recent years Mexico City has been able to collect nearly 50 per cent of all property taxes in Mexico. This pattern of fiscal concentration is also visible in the city itself, where four of Mexico City's sixteen boroughs account for nearly 60 per cent of the locally collected property taxes. These boroughs are Cuauthémoc, Miguel Hidalgo, Benito Juárez and Alvaro Obregón (Bird and Slack 2008: 151). The fact that Cuauthémoc is at the top of this list points towards the spatial implications of the city's urban development strategy. The borough comprises large parts of the city's historic centre, which due to its colonial architecture and central location seems to be a more than promising area for attracting international capital in fields such as heritage tourism and real estate development – and for generating local tax revenue. However, due to the growing spatial concentration of urban marginality and informality in downtown Mexico City, both the local business community as well as the PRD administrations increasingly considered the historic centre as an endangered urban area, most of all, because the spatial condensation of urban marginality in this area 'has prevented the city authorities from capitalizing on the area's tourism potential. [...] Consequently, some business groups in the area, as well as city authorities, have expressed serious concern about street vending. The Historic Center is said to be in crisis' (Crossa 2009: 47). Confronted with this situation that potentially threatens the economic development potential of the historic centre, local businessmen increasingly started to intervene in public debates in order to move the local government towards action. In a strategy paper published in 2001, which in a paradigmatic way illustrates the securitization of urban space that accompanies the urbanization of neoliberalism in the city, the influential private business council, the Consejo Coordinador Empresarial (Empresarial Coordination Council, CCE) stated that,

> [T]he Historic Centre is being lumpenized [*lumpenizado*] and occupied by the excluded who view the run-down monumentality as an opportunity for cheap housing and protection for informal and delinquent activities. The housing conditions in the Historic Centre as well as its competitiveness to attract investments deteriorate, [...]. Informality nourishes and protects illegal, vandalistic conducts and irregular appropriations of public spaces. Laws are dead letters, the state withdraws from regulation. Chaotic transport, street commerce, political demonstrations and protest camps, rubbish, fiscal evasions, brothels and prostitution challenge and subdue the state. A culture of illegality is being reproduced and ever more firmly rooted, and so is a new mafia power that draws on old and new corporatist and clientelistic vices. (CCE/CESPEDES 2001: 10–11)

In order to confront this crisis, a public–private partnership emerged that brought to town zero tolerance policing, the core element of urban revanchism (see introduction), in the guise of a contract with Giuliani Partners, the security consultancy founded by former New York City mayor and 'inventor' of zero tolerance policing, Rudolph Giuliani. This decision was facilitated by the discursive arrival of zero tolerance during the first PRD administration and its efforts to demonstrate that the party was taking the local crime problems seriously (see below).

Moreover, as Chapter 4 will demonstrate, local think tanks, NGOs and 'philanthropic' foundations like México Unido Contra la Delincuencia actively participated in the diffusion of zero tolerance ideas, thereby contributing to the merging of a neoliberal political economy symbolized by the 'Chicago Boys' and an economy of 'security' expertise promoted by the 'New York Boys', most notably Rudolph Giuliani and his Police Chief William Bratton (Wacquant 2009a: 167–168). This merger did not happen by accident, but was in fact the main objective of the Giuliani initiative 'because it was tacitly understood [by the city administration and the private sector] that Giuliani would propose policies whose most tangible effect would be to help foster downtown real estate development and speed the "rescue" of historic Mexico City' (Davis 2013: 61). Related policy proposals were provided with the Giuliani report, which was presented to the public in August 2003 (on the Giuliani initiative, see Becker and Müller 2013; Müller 2009a, 2012c: 138–148, 2013a; Campesi 2010: 458–460; Davis 2013; Mitchell and Beckett 2008; Mountz and Curran 2009).

The report, unsurprisingly, promotes the security efforts 'that have been successful in New York', including 'the Broken Windows approach of George Kelling', as 'the model for police action' in Mexico City (SSPDF 2003: 5). As '[c]rime is frequently a symptom of societal decay', it is recommended that local policing should primarily 'target the roots of crime problems (drugs, vagrancy, etc.) and seek long term efficient solutions' (ibid.: 46). In this regard, the strict enforcement and prosecution of public nuisance offences are presented as 'decisive questions for the quality of life of the inhabitants', in particular because 'the [policing] strategy adopted in this city during the last decade has been exactly the opposite of the "broken windows" doctrine' (ibid.: 36). In order to move local policing in the right direction, it is furthermore recommended that the local laws be subject to a revision, because they would often provide the police with insufficient authorization for effectively confronting the problems threatening the local 'quality of life' (ibid.: 42). According to the report, the latter is most of all threatened by the city's growing informal economy: 'During the last years, the number of people that have converted public spaces into their work place has exceptionally multiplied. Be it "franeleros" who block parking spaces with objects in order to later charge for their use, or "*limpia-parabrisas*" [squeegee cleaners] who impose an unsolicited service. It is a fact that both cases represent a problem for the inhabitants of the city' (ibid.: 39). Other activities that allegedly threaten the quality of life in Mexico City include graffiti – considered as an 'aggression against the collective patrimony' (ibid.: 38) – sex work, the presence of street children, noise and public drinking (ibid.: 39–40). As all of these practices are primarily visible in public spaces, the 'recuperation of public spaces' plays a central role in the Giuliani report. Among other aspects, this includes a plea for the architectural 'modification of public spaces in criminogenic areas' (ibid.: 11), as well as the massive implementation of closed-circuit television (CCTV) surveillance in areas particularly subject to the threat of crime and graffiti (ibid.: 38).

Many of the report's recommendations were integrated into the previously mentioned *rescue project*. In fact, a central objective of the project, according to official discourse, is to 'reduce criminality in the Historic Center and to promote our city as a tourist location and to recover the confidence of the citizenry and the visitors by means of concrete and coordinated actions' (SSPDF 2006: 250). Regarding the influence of the Giuliani report on the rescue project, the latter, for instance, included the creation of the so-called Citizen Protection Units (CPUs), operating along a 'proximity policing scheme' (ibid.: 147), evidently mixing zero tolerance policing with community policing, as recommended by the Giuliani report (SSPDF 2003: 40). Three of the first four CPUs were installed in the Zócalo, Paseo de la Reforma and Alameda, all areas in the historic centre that attract most of the political, economic and tourist attention. The same holds true for the installation of CCTV cameras, another of the Giuliani report's recommendations. The first cameras were installed in the so-called Financial-Tourist Corridor of the historic centre in 2002, while since then the CCTV coverage of the area has been permanently expanded. This is part 'of a strategy of securitization that seeks to establish a logic of monitoring, classification and control of the population's movements' (Arteaga Botello 2013: 231), in particular within the context of the 'Bicenntenial Project: Safe City'. The latter has been implemented by the administration of Marcelo Ebrard (2006–2012), Mexico City's former police chief during whose tenure the Giuliani report was published, within the context of the Bicentennial of Mexico's Independence in 2010. The goal of the project was to transform Mexico City into one of the safest cities in the world through the installation of 12,000 surveillance cameras (ibid.: 237).

In addition to these technological aspects, the recommendations of the Giuliani report have also been incorporated into the new urban design of public spaces in the historic centre, which was inspired by Barcelona's urban renewal effort, specifically by the creation of 'hard plazas', that is concrete-based open public spaces that are austerely equipped and removed of trees, plants or green surfaces (Herzog 2003: 293). In the adaptation of this concept to Mexico City, the topic of visibility and order became a central concern that directly linked urban design to security and surveillance objectives, implying the removal of all kinds of disturbing signposts, the cutting down and reordering of trees and the planting of non-exuberant species with the aim of facilitating surveillance of the 'rescued' public spaces and the prevention of the presence of undesired practices and people.

Despite the fact that local politicians and police chiefs frequently distanced themselves publicly from zero tolerance policing, and the Giuliani initiative in general, the impact of these tactics and their translation into a 'quality of life' policing effort by the local police forces is undeniable, as the following passage taken from an interview with the police chief of the First Region (historic centre) and his personal assistant demonstrates:

Many of Giuliani's recommendations certainly shaped the security program for the historic centre. It's what we have just said about the Broken Windows Theory. That is to say, that as long as the space is clean and remains recuperated, we will impede or prevent delinquency. [...] With regard to the recuperation of space, it is the task of the Secretary of Public Security to permit the flow of traffic [*hacer las calles transitadas*] by means of the Civic Culture Law, which forms part of Giuliani's recommendations to improve the urban environment, to make people aware that this space is a space for all, that is, it must be a habitable space, and that you have to respect it. [...] The Civic Culture Law is also applied in the case of the obstruction of public space by the informal commerce and by *franeleros* in order to improve the traffic regulation in the area, thereby contributing to more secure spaces and making people feel that they are in a spacious place and can freely circulate, that a delinquent may not hide behind a car.

The implementation of these social control and surveillance efforts, aimed at the spatial displacement of urban marginality and informality that the securitization processes unfolding in downtown Mexico City portray as risks, is, however, inseparable from the invention of new legal instruments that criminalize urban marginality, such as the Civic Culture Law mentioned by the interviewee.

Lawfare à la Mexicana

A central element of the punitive government of urban marginality in neoliberal Mexico City consists of a particular 'mobilization of legalities' that the Comaroffs call 'lawfare'. With this term, they describe 'the resort to legal instruments, to the violence inherent in the law, to commit acts of political coercion, even erasure' (Comaroff and Comaroff 2006: 30). Lawfare, in this regard, is a core element of 'rule through law' (Hathazy and Müller 2016; see also Rajkovic 2010). This term designates the conversion of the 'impartial character of law and legal processes into political means that, by criminalizing certain practices most often associated with people at society's margins, aim at enhancing the legitimacy of political actors through practices of legal-political exclusion' (Hathazy and Müller 2016: 116).

The most important element within the arsenal of local lawfare tools is another outcome of the Giuliani report, the Civic Culture Law of the Federal District (LCC), referred to above. The LCC was enacted in 2004, and justified by the local administration with exactly the same arguments and objectives as those mentioned in the Giuliani report: the punishment of activities that 'promote disorder' in the city and 'attack the quality of life' (*La Jornada* 2004c).

Despite the seemingly emancipatory language of the law that recognizes the city's cultural diversity and that employs the term 'citizen security' instead of 'public security', while simultaneously presenting itself as a contribution to a 'harmonious cohabitation' in the city (Article 2), the LCC's inspiration by the broken windows theory and zero tolerance policing is clearly evident. The LCC presents a total of forty-three minor offences (administrative infractions) punishable by monetary fines of 1–30 days' earnings of the minimum wage or confinement between six and thirty-six hours. Examples of such minor offences are 'providing a service without it having been solicited', 'invitation to or performance of prostitution as well as soliciting this service' or 'to block the entrance to public buildings while offering to provide administrative services without official authorization', all of which are considered to be 'violations of the peace or privacy of persons'. In addition, the 'consumption of alcoholic beverages in public spaces where the consumption of alcohol has not been authorized' is classified as a violation of 'citizen security'. Other activities, such as graffiti, or to be more precise, the 'damaging, painting, besmirching or inappropriate use of the walls of public or private buildings, statues, monuments, signs, street lights', are considered to be 'infractions against the urban environment' (Articles 23–26).

The enactment of the LCC had immediate consequences for the urban marginals struggling to make a living in the informal economy on the streets of downtown Mexico City. Just one week after the enactment of the law, the public was informed that there are up to 340 daily arrests of *franeleros*. One year later, a daily average of 231 persons were arrested in Mexico City due to infractions of the LLC, a number that by 2006 had already increased to a total of 408.6 persons, mostly *franeleros* and *limpia-parabrisas*, due to the obstruction and/or blocking of public spaces (Becker and Müller 2013: 83) – an arrest pattern that, as will be shown below, continues into the present. Additionally, the LCC contributed to an increase in detentions of and police violence against local sex workers, another segment of the informal urban economy whose presence on the streets of Mexico City seems to be at odds with the creation of an investment-friendly urban environment. Already in 2004, there were 2,378 arrests based on violations of the LCC by sex workers (Becker and Müller 2011: 66–67). Moreover, the LCC's commitment to the 'recuperation of public spaces' and the improvement of the local 'quality of life' directly translated into the 14,331 arrests that accompanied the removal of street vendors in October 2007 from the 192 blocks of the historic centre (SSPDF 2008).

Another element within the local arsenal of lawfare tools is the Extinction of Property Law of the Federal District (LED). The origins of the LED can be traced back to two expropriations of real estate properties in spring 2007. One of the properties was a low-income block located in the Tepito neighbourhood, whose residents were allegedly involved in organized criminal activities, such as kidnapping, drug trafficking and product piracy. While the fight against organized crime featured prominently in the official discourse justifying the expropriation, it must be kept in mind that the expropriation was also related to a larger pacification strategy that aimed at disciplining the neighbourhood's informal economy, an important step towards the planned integration of the area into the urban renewal process in downtown Mexico City (Campesi 2010: 461), which will be analysed in detail in Chapter 3. The legal basis for this expropriation, however, was not the LED but 'a legal tool justified by the spirit of the new health regulation as the basis for securitizing the city, with the aim being to remove *narcomenudeo* [small-scale drug trafficking]' (Davis and Ruiz de Teresa 2013: 118). The other expropriation took place in Iztapalapa, one of the most marginalized boroughs of the city. Here, the target was a property locally known as '*predio Ford*', where car parts, frequently of illegal origin, could be purchased. Leaving aside the cases of police abuse that accompanied the expropriations – and which were widely covered by the local media – one particular problem for the local government was the weak legal basis of these actions and the accusation, for instance, by the Human Rights Commission of the Federal District (CDHDF), that the expropriations were illegal (*El Universal* 2007a). In this regard, the local administration searched for international legal innovations that would legalize the expropriations, and, following the path of Colombian criminal politics, in December 2008, the LED was enacted (see also Davis and Ruiz de Teresa 2013: 123–125). The law permits the immediate intervention of judicial authorities in order to confiscate real estate property on the basis of indications that a building is being used for activities classified as organized crime. The law was spectacularly inaugurated in the historic centre in March 2009 with the expropriation of three buildings in the marginalized Merced neighbourhood, which due to its historical architecture became the focus of the expansion of the urban renewal project in downtown Mexico City under the administration of Marcelo Ebrard (see Chapter 3).

The legal targeting of undesirable informal economic activities – and urban marginality in general – through the LCC and LED created a punitive topography, clearly visible in the spatial bias of the resulting law enforcement measures. As the latter predominantly focus upon spaces of economic interest for real estate development and urban renewal projects in downtown Mexico City, these laws have converted many places in which the urban marginals live and struggle for economic survival into veritable 'spatial containers for the ostracization of undesirable social categories and activities' (Wacquant 2008b: 11) – an undesirability largely derived from the obstacles the physical presence of the 'urban outcasts' is imagined to represent for the global competitiveness of the city's economy. However, in contrast to what Wacquant observed for the rolling-out of the penal state in the US and Western Europe, the economic contribution of the punitive governance of urban marginality in Mexico City does not primarily consist of its capacity to discipline the lower segments of the local working class 'by raising the cost of strategies of resistance to desocialized wage labor via "exit" into the informal economy' (Wacquant 2009b: 80). Rather, in the near absence of any formal employment opportunities for the urban marginals, the criminalization of urban poverty that accompanies the securitization of urban space serves the real and symbolic disciplining – including spatial displacement – of the informal economy in order to enhance the city's attractiveness as an investment location within growing global inter-urban competition.

Although the local penalization of marginality is in this regard inseparable from the neoliberal restructuring of the city's economy, the former received an additional impetus from legal changes and securitization processes at the national level (on the latter, see Müller 2016a). Here, it must be recalled that Mexican penal legislation differentiates between local laws and federal laws. Federal laws, in general, relate to more serious criminal activities such as terrorism or organized crime. The perception of the seriousness of particular criminal activities, however, was substantially altered during and after the North American Free Trade Agreement (NAFTA) negotiation process, as can be seen within the realm of intellectual property rights. In order to comply with its NAFTA obligations and those from the World Intellectual Property Organization, Mexico's first two post-PRI governments – those of Vicente Fox Quesada (2000–2006) and Felipe Calderón Hinojosa (2006–2012), both belonging to the PAN – enacted a variety of legal instruments and strengthened existing ones in order to enforce intellectual copyright violations more thoroughly. Contemporary legislation defines the profit-oriented illegal reproduction of copyright-protected products, such as movies, music or software, as a federal crime that is punishable by up to ten years in prison or up to 10,000 days' earnings of the minimum wage (Aguiar 2012: 168; Cross 2007: 126). Considering that in all of its country reports on Mexico, the International Intellectual Copyright Alliance mentions Mexico City, in particular Tepito, as the most notorious place for the violation of intellectual property rights in the country, it is of little surprise that the neighbourhood, as will be shown in Chapter 3, has increasingly become the object of police raids. However, as a growing segment of the urban workforce is increasingly excluded from the formal job market, producing and vending pirated DVDs and CDs on the streets of Mexico City is one of the few viable strategies for ensuring the socio-economic reproduction of entire families (Cross 2007: 137). In this regard, national-level compliance with the prerogatives of the global neoliberal copyright regime added another dimension to the penalization of poverty in urban Mexico, clearly visible in the fact that copyright-related police operations increased from only four in 2000 to 8,753 in 2006 (Aguiar 2012: 167), further contributing to the criminalization of neighbourhoods like Tepito and their residents by adding a *'blemish of place'* (Wacquant 2007: 67, original emphasis) to the already existing patterns of sociopolitical marginalization – and criminalization – that residents of these areas are confronted with in their daily lives.

Punitive democratization

Following the implementation of NAFTA, and the economic crisis of 1994, Mexico City witnessed a hitherto unparalleled rise in street crime, in particular assaults, robberies and petty theft. According to official statistics, crime rates declined after the late 1990s, but they never returned to the pre-crisis levels (Pansters and Castillo Berthier 2007: 43). However, even if crime in contemporary Mexico City is higher than it was before 1994 and the city has the highest victimization rates in the country, with nearly 20 per cent of its residents having suffered a crime in 2008 (Koonings and Kruijt 2015b: 42), the widespread 'climate of fear' in the city cannot be reduced to criminal insecurity. As argued in the introduction, crime and insecurity have been part and parcel of modern Mexico City's urban reality. The more recent climate of fear and urban anxiety reflects, as Gutman reminds us, 'a general sense of helplessness' that has been unfolding since the mid-1990s, in response to 'frustration over elections that seemed to accomplish nothing, an ebbing of social movements throughout the country, and a dramatic decline in purchasing power following the financial crisis in 1994–95' (Gutman 2006: 141). Even though the widespread climate of fear in Mexico City cannot exclusively be explained with rising criminal insecurity, through its discursive reworking and amplification within the journalistic field and public opinion polls, this climate of anxiety increasingly defined the discursive parameters of local urban politics, producing another securitization process which converted crime into the single most important issue on the urban political agenda (Castillo 2008: 181).

This situation threatens the legitimacy and symbolic authority of the local state as the ultimate authority in charge of providing security for its subjects, a challenge that is related to the local government's official redefinition of security as *public security* in the mid-1990s, which made it clear to the city's residents that security was no longer about regime protection but the provision of a public good (see Müller 2014). While the blame for the security crisis of the mid-1990s could be placed on the authoritarian policing legacy that characterized the seven decades of PRI rule in Mexico City during which policing was synonymous with regime protection, in the eyes of many local residents, the PRD has yet to demonstrate how democratic urban politics actually make a difference in terms of improving local security and for living up to the proclaimed standards of security as a public good. In order to respond to this challenge, the PRD adopted a political strategy that aimed at 'the ritual reassertion of the sovereignty of the state in the narrow, *theatricalized domain of law enforcement that it has prioritized for that very purpose*' (Wacquant 2009a: 299, original emphasis).

It is frequently assumed that when, in 1997, Cárdenas was democratically elected as the city's first mayor since 1928, his administration struggled to improve the security situation in the city and to transform and democratize local law enforcement. However, at a closer look, the PRD's security policies have, from the very start, been far more ambivalent than many observers suggest. For example, while the related literature discusses the import of zero tolerance policing nearly exclusively with reference to the López Obrador and Ebrard administrations (see the references above), it must be recalled that it was Cárdenas who, in the wake of the 1997 election, brought the punitive discourse of zero tolerance to Mexico City. For instance, in December of that year, the then-chief of the judicial police, Tornero Salinas, publicly declared that 'the instructions of the head of government, Cuauthémoc Cárdenas and Attorney General Samuel del Villar, are to prosecute delinquents under the principal of "zero tolerance," but within the realm of legality and full respect for the human rights of both, victim and perpetrator' (*La Jornada* 1997). Del Villar even travelled to New York to get some first-hand advice on zero tolerance and how to implement it in Mexico City (Arteaga Botello 2004: 195, fn. 41). This commitment to zero tolerance was also shared by Cárdenas' police chief, Debernardi. Upon taking office, he publicly declared that he would reduce local crime rates within three months by adopting New York-style zero tolerance policing (López-Montiel 2000: 88).

While the full-fledged implementation of zero tolerance policing still had to wait for a couple of years, the discursive arrival of zero tolerance coincided with the democratization of local politics under PRD rule, showing that, as elsewhere (Wacquant 2009b: 23), leftist parties are not immune to the symbolic seduction of the zero tolerance 'success story', a story whose import by the Cárdenas administration also served the purpose of symbolically assuring Mexico City residents (and voters) that the local government is in fact doing everything it can to improve the security situation. This symbolic strategy also included proposals to toughen existing laws along the lines of broken windows/zero tolerance, as the following public statement by del Villar demonstrates in a paradigmatic way:

> Street crime breeds from antisocial behaviour that undermines public order and that is not vigorously defined in the Penal Code. [...] The security of the population demands that the Penal Code

recognizes order, respect and public spaces as legally protected goods and sanctions, for instance, those who beat up persons; consume alcoholic beverages or narcotics in public spaces and get together for this purpose; operate a vehicle under the influence of alcohol or of narcotics; vandalize in public or in public transport without adequate permit or license. (DDLDB 1999: 60–61)

Although the proposed legal reforms were only implemented with the enactment of the LCC in 2004, it is nonetheless remarkable that all PRD administrations, beginning with Cárdenas, while publicly declaring the fight against crime as being closely related to the fight against poverty (see also Arteaga Botello 2004: 231–239), shared a punitive commitment that converted democratic policing in Mexico City right from the start into an ambivalent affair. Driven by the double pressure of rebuilding the symbolic authority of the local state and demonstrating that the PRD is actually making a difference in terms of local policing, the PRD's security policies converted the most marginalized segments of the population, which also represent the party's main electoral constituency, into the principal targets of democratic law enforcement. This outcome is also related to efforts of extending the PRD's electoral base beyond the urban poor and the ideologically left-leaning members of the middle class through a publicly visible commitment to middle- and upper-class security concerns. As these concerns are largely centred on issues such as car theft or the proper use of urban space, the PRD's efforts of demonstrating that the party is taking these matters seriously translates into more police presence in middle-class neighbourhoods as well as the surveillance and frequent expulsion of 'undesirable' people – the urban marginals – from such places (Müller 2012c: 165–166). This has been accompanied by other theatrical police interventions, such as the expropriation of the *predio Ford*' in Iztapalapa referred to above.

This symbolic strengthening of state and party through a theatricalization of law enforcement, however, is not only related to a zero tolerance-oriented discursive criminalization of poverty. It has also been accompanied by a public celebration of punishment, a related toughening of local penal laws – culminating in a recent reform proposal of the penal code by then mayor Ebrard, which includes a plea for up to thirty years of imprisonment for people disturbing the 'social peace' in the city (*La Jornada* 2012), the political discovery of the 'crime victim' (Wacquant 2008b: 10) as well as the declaration of a democratic right to punish. In regards to the latter, for instance, the 2000–2006 General Development Plan for the Federal District, the city's main policy planning instrument, stated that the local democratic order is an order essentially based upon punishment: 'The democratic order not only consists of the representative character of the public authorities and citizen participation, but also of the certainty that delinquent behavior will be sanctioned' (PGDDF 2000: 36).

As the most convincing way to demonstrate such certainty is the presentation of statistical evidence, it is hardly surprising that the local police introduced a detention quota in 2005, providing 'efficient' police officers with financial (and promotional) bonuses if they fulfil a certain number of detentions a year. In 2006, the local police aimed at an annual detention quota of 27,300 persons (Jiménez Ornelas and Moreno Alva 2007: 198). This quota added another dimension to the criminalization of poverty in Mexico City as it converted the most vulnerable segments of the urban poor, particularly marginalized youth, into the principal victims of this strategy of symbolically legitimizing the local state and the PRD through a policing-by-numbers effort. This went hand in hand with a 'moral panic' about street gangs in Mexico City, which are blamed for urban violence and social breakdown, in particular in the more marginalized parts of the city. Convinced that gangs 'kill, rob, rape and produce fear', the local government tried to impede gang formation through so-called 'Dispan' police operations, which in Spanish stands for *dispersión de pandillas* (gang dispersion) (Castillo Berthier and Jones 2009: 187). As elsewhere in Latin America, such tactics reflect a tendency to blame 'gangs and other unsavoury segments of the population' for the social dislocations and insecurities that accompanied the unfolding of neoliberalism (Thomas et al. 2011: 2). As a result of this, aesthetics that could potentially indicate one's belonging to a deviant and dangerous youth culture, such as having a tattoo or wearing the wrong clothes converts marginal youth immediately into suspects for the local police (Müller 2012d: 329–330). The resulting everyday punitive exposure of marginal youth in Mexico City is further aggravated by Mexico's war on drugs and the related militarization of law enforcement. In contemporary Mexico City, the punitive character of the urban democracy, in combination with the national anti-drug crusade, created a context in which it is very likely that 'when a young person is stopped with paints in a rucksack it will be by a municipal officer keen to demonstrate his grasp of "zero tolerance"; possession of fireworks will bring attention of the AFI [Federal Investigative Agency]; and antidrug raids at clubs are more likely to involve actual or former military personnel' (Castillo Berthier and Jones 2009: 198). Against this background, from the perspective of the penal experience of the urban poor, the democratization of Mexico City politics indicates a remarkable continuity with authoritarian practices under PRI rule (see also Campesi 2010), with the important difference being that police repression has shifted from the 'enemies of the revolution' towards an enemy represented by the undesirable urban 'other'. These processes continue into the present under Ebrard's successor, Miguel Ángel Mancera (PRD), who increasingly resorts to lawfare practices in an effort to confront opposition movements in the city (Müller 2016a: 239). For instance, in responding to a rising number of violent clashes between police and protestors at manifestations and rallies, his administration modified Articles 123, 130, 224 and 241 of the local penal code. The reformed articles now nearly double prison terms for violence directed against public authorities during demonstrations (*El Universal* 2013), thereby actively reinforcing authoritarian tendencies that criminalize political opposition and civic protest against PRD rule in the city.

The consequences of punitive democratization

The remaining parts of this chapter will examine the everyday practices of the main institutions in charge of the punitive governing of urban marginality in contemporary Mexico City in order to provide some insights regarding the resulting consequences for the people subject to them. In particular, I will turn to the role of policing, court practices, the prison system and the role of social assistance programmes in penalizing marginality in contemporary Mexico City.

Policing urban marginality

The preceding sections have already demonstrated that, as in other cities that witnessed the emergence of 'advanced marginality', the Mexico City police have been entrusted 'with buttressing the new social order woven out of vertiginous inequalities and with checking the turbulences born of the explosive conjunction of rampant poverty and stupendous affluence engendered by neoliberal capitalism' (Wacquant 2008b: 12). As recent work on Latin American policing has shown throughout the region, the practices of urban police forces are marked by widespread corruption, abusive and violent behaviour – including extralegal killings – and collusion with criminal actors (e.g. Arias and Goldstein 2010; Moreira Alves and Evanson 2011; O'Neill and Thomas 2011). Mexico City is no exception in this regard. Although the absence of military rule has probably spared the city from the militaristic self-imagination of urban police forces that continues to haunt policing practices in countries of the Southern Cone – frequently leading to widespread extralegal police killings of urban marginals (Stanley 2010) – routine, but rarely lethal, police violence, is a common feature of local law enforcement (Azaola and Ruiz Torres 2011; Silva 2007; Uildriks 2010). According to a representative survey, in 2005, about 760,000 of a total of 1,680,000 cases of contact between Mexico City residents and the local police involved some form of police abuse. While the overwhelming majority of abuse was non-physical and involved some kind of extortion, the survey nonetheless indicates that some 70,000 cases of physical abuse were committed by the local law enforcement agencies in this period (Naval 2006: 21). In light of these numbers, the criminalization of poverty in contemporary Mexico City increasingly exposes the urban poor to the threat of violent police behaviour. While it is true that through bribery as well as informal negotiations and clientelist exchanges, local law enforcement is – and has always been – a matter of negotiation (on this issue see Müller 2012c), the emergence of the punitive city has increasingly raised the costs for the affected people to bargain over the non-enforcement of laws and to engage in rule-bending practices with local brokers and police agents. On the one hand, the introduction of detention quotas and the related financial reward and promotion system for police officers (see above) has raised the financial stakes for the urban poor to bribe their way out of detention. On the other hand, due to the enactment of new laws that criminalize urban poverty, such as the LCC, the urban marginals have become increasingly dependent upon the help of brokers to protect them from the enforcement of these laws by the local authorities (see Chapter 2). However, as such protection frequently also involves financial payments, those who cannot afford such monetary investments, or those without any connections to brokers at all, for instance marginalized youth and street children, are the ones most likely to suffer the full repressive weight of the local penal state.

Civic judges

As argued above, the LCC serves as the dominant legal tool for the punitive governing of urban marginality in contemporary Mexico City. As infractions of the LCC are defined as administrative offences, the main institution responsible for punishing violations of the LCC are the civic judges (*juzgados cívicos*), not the Attorney General. According to existing legislation, as soon as a person is arrested by the police for violating the LCC, the person must immediately be transferred to one of the city's fifty-nine civic judges who determines the sentences, ranging from the simple issuing of a warning, to community work, to paying a fine or arrest, although arrest and monetary fines are the predominant sanctions. In May 2001, the CDHDF issued a recommendation to the city administration requesting the improvement of the facilities and administrative routines of the civic judges, which in many ways violated the rights of those arrested, notably due to widespread abuse of detainees, unhealthy arrest conditions and the lack of basic sanitary infrastructure (CDHDF 2001). Four years later, following the enactment of the LCC, the CDHDF followed up on this recommendation and published a full report on the civic judges. The document provides ample evidence regarding ongoing human rights violations in this area of the local administration of justice, including, for instance, abuse and physical mistreatment of arrested persons, reported by 19 per cent of the detainees (CDHDF 2005: 25), the absence of an assigned counsel in 70 per cent of all cases (ibid.: 34) and not providing food (in 86 per cent of all cases) and water (in 53 per cent of all cases) for arrested persons (ibid.: 50). The report furthermore stresses that, in particular, people living in a situation of high vulnerability, like minors – arrested in 17 per cent of all cases for playing soccer on the streets – elderly persons or sick people, suffer disproportionately under the abovementioned deficient infrastructure and arbitrary/abusive practices (ibid.: 55–62). Reflecting the 'quality of life' focus of the LCC, the report also indicates that 56 per cent of the arrested persons were detained because of drinking in public spaces, drug use (19 per cent), urinating in public spaces (9 per cent), illegal use of public spaces (8 per cent), offences against the 'social cohabitation in public spaces' (4 per cent), violent behaviour (2 per cent) and prostitution (1 per cent) (ibid.: 32).

When considering that the CDHDF had to admit in a more recent statement that most of these problems within the realm of civic justice continue to exist (*El Universal* 2008), it must be assumed that the steady increase in the number of people arrested due to violations of the LCC has aggravated these problems. In fact, the number of persons brought before the civic judges nearly tripled between 2006 and 2011, rising from 49,205 to 134,731 (CJSL 2011: 55). When unpacking these numbers, the correlation between the urbanization of neoliberalism, the securitization of urban space and the criminalization of poverty in Mexico City becomes evident. Official statistics clearly demonstrate that, in spatial terms, the borough with the highest number of arrests due to infractions of the LCC is Cuauhtémoc, the borough in which the historic centre is located. In this borough, 56,719 arrested persons were brought before the civic judges between August 2010 and September 2011 due to LCC-related infractions, nearly half of all cases reported in Mexico City for this period (CJSL 2011: 56). Moreover, official statistics also show that 30,701 of the cases brought before the civic judges were related to informal economic activities that obstructed public spaces, and another 40,005 to public drinking (ibid.: 57). In light of this scenario, it becomes apparent that the civic judges have indeed complied with their official mission of 'calling attention to behaviour that is pernicious to society' (ibid.: 57). This perniciousness is defined in the risk urban marginality poses to the neo-liberal vision of urban order and, as in the case of local policing, the punitive containment of the former through the activities of the civic judges exposes a growing number of the city's most disadvantaged residents to arbitrary, unhealthy and illegal penal practices.

The prison system

In 1991, Human Rights Watch, after visiting Mexican prisons, including facilities in Mexico City, published a detailed report that identified a variety of the local prison system's structural problems, including massive overcrowding, corruption and abuse by prison personnel as well as a general lack of resources (HRW 1991: 47). By that time, prisons in authoritarian PRI Mexico housed some 88,000 inmates (ibid.: vii). This number increased to some 139,000 in 1999 (Azaola and Bergman 2007: 100), the year before the electoral victory of Vicente Fox Quesada that marked the widely recognized democratic breakthrough at the national level. In June 2012, after more than a decade of democratization, the number of inmates had nearly doubled. Currently, some 237,566 people are imprisoned in Mexico (Presidencia de la República 2012: 32). To put it in other terms, democratic Mexico has put more people behind bars than its authoritarian predecessor. A similar development can be observed in Mexico City. In 1993, the year before the 'security crisis' of 1994, Mexico City had a prison population of 8,472 inmates. This number even decreased to 8,361 in 1995. One year before the 1997 elections that brought the PRD to power, Mexico City's prisons housed some 11,042 inmates. One year after the PRD's electoral victory, this number had already increased to 16,989. In 2000, the inmate population had further grown to 21,857 persons (Ruiz Ortega 2006: 4). This trend of a rising inmate population has continued into the present, with 42,297 people being held in one of Mexico City's ten prison facilities in September 2012. As their national counterparts, the democratic governments in Mexico City, despite declining crime rates (see above) have put more people behind bars than their authoritarian PRI predecessors. When taking a closer look at the composition of the prison population, it becomes apparent that the overwhelming majority of inmates (84 per cent) are imprisoned due to infractions of local laws, not federal ones combating organized crime and drug trafficking (CDHDF 2011: 11). Moreover, the overwhelming majority of local inmates are imprisoned for minor property crimes that qualify as informal economic survival strategies, like robbery (nearly 70 per cent of all inmates), in general below a value of 2,000 Pesos (about US$200) (Bergman et al. 2006: 39). Simple robbery, due to the strengthening of existing penal laws, is currently punished with a prison sentence ranging from three to ten years (Dammert and Zúñiga 2008: 35) and the average sentence for a prisoner – excluding those who have committed a homicide – in Mexico City is 8.4 years (Bergman et al. 2006: 31). Reflecting the negative consequences of the rolling-out of the penal state for the most disadvantaged segments of the local population, most inmates belong to the urban marginals whose life outside prison has been dominated by permanent conditions of 'unemployment, informality and marginality' (ibid.: 26). In this regard, in Mexico City, as well as in the country as a whole, 'inmates are generally not the most dangerous criminals, but they are the poorest' (Azaola and Bergman 2007: 112).

As in the other institutions in charge of implementing punitive politics in Mexico City, and this brings us back to the Human Rights Watch report, the conditions in which inmates have to live inside the local prison system continue to violate basic human rights and existing legal standards. To begin with, all prison facilities in Mexico City suffer from massive overcrowding, which is openly acknowledged on the website of the Sub-secretariat for the Penitentiary System. In fact, Mexico City prisons are the most overpopulated correctional facilities in the entire country, with overpopulation rates reaching about 96 per cent (Dammert and Zúñiga 2008: 42). This overpopulation has increased the serious deficiencies inside the local prison system that, as academic studies as well as reports by CDHDF demonstrate, have not substantially improved since the Human Rights Watch visit in the early 1990s. Abuse and violence among inmates and by the prison guards is common, sanitary and health conditions are deficient, as is the provision of food and drinking water, leading to the fact that inmates' families have to purchase food, clothes and other basic items, which frequently involves bribing the guards (Azaola and Bergman 2007: 105–106; Bergman et al. 2006: 41–51; CDHDF 2011, 2005). This is another indication that neoliberal democratization in Mexico City did not imply a rupture with those institutional problems that haunted the penal apparatus under authoritarian one-party rule.

Securitizing welfare

Mexico City is often credited with having 'more extensive and generous welfare programs than those implemented nationally' and with 'the aspiration of Mexico City's government to develop its own social policy which has the explicit aim of guaranteeing social rights for the city's inhabitants' (Hudson and Medrano 2013: 4). This aspiration is part of a city branding initiative through which the PRD is trying to promote Mexico's capital as an inclusive city, a 'city of hope' (*ciudad de la esperanza*). The expansion of social assistance programmes by the PRD governments, however, as in other Latin American contexts, does not stand in contrast to the more general punitive turn in local politics but is an integral element of the latter. First of all, these social programmes have been deeply embedded in an expansion of clientelist relations that accompanied the local democratization process (see Chapter 2). This development consolidated another element within the punitive techniques of the governing of marginality in the city that, following Auyero, can be called 'clandestine kicks'. With this notion, Auyero refers to the 'illegal exercise of violence carried out by actors connected with established powerholders' in their efforts to control urban marginality (Auyero 2012: 15). The concept of clandestine kicks, however, can be extended beyond the realm of physical violence to include the intentional, and equally punitive, withholding/politicized granting of social services on the calculation of the recipients' political loyalty. In this regard, the extension of social assistance programmes through clientelist channels includes a strong penalizing component against disloyal clients, which further contributes to the punitive governing of urban marginality in the city within the sphere of informal politics (as will be demonstrated in greater detail in the next chapter).

Moreover, and more broadly, social assistance and welfare programmes as Verónica Schild (2015) has shown, do not stand in opposition to the general punitive turn in the region. They are, in reality, one of its core elements, which explains the simultaneous expansion of lawfare, prisonfare *and* welfare efforts in Latin American penal state formation mentioned in the introduction to this book (see also Müller 2012a). The punitive governing of urban marginality in contemporary Latin America, Schild points out, not only takes the form of lawfare and a policing-centred criminalization of poverty, it also includes ameliorative policies, welfare programs – in particular conditional cash transfer programmes – and targeted social assistance initiatives that have become integrated into the overall securitization agenda that underpins neoliberal state practices throughout the region:

> Overcoming poverty seems to be rapidly overshadowed by the question of security, and the concern with securing the so-called 'vulnerable' by targeting the neediest through novel social programs and modest expansions in health and pension coverage seems to be interrelated to the restructuring of the penal system, including judicial and police reforms, and the expansion of prisons. (Schild 2015: 5)

Under these circumstances, many welfare programmes in Latin America, far from being impartial and disinterested forms of empowerment and poverty reduction, are essential means for the management of 'social and political instability in the present Latin American capitalist contexts' (ibid.: 44) by confronting the risk those at urban society's margins represent for political stability and the attractiveness of investment locations for globally mobile capital – a fact that also explains the renaissance of population-centric counterinsurgency approaches that are presented as armed social work in places like Brazil, Haiti or Guatemala (Müller 2016b; Hochmüller and Müller 2016).

In Mexico City, social assistance programmes like Prepa Sí ('high school, yes') – an educational 'incentive programme' (*programa de estímulos*) targeting teenagers to reduce dropout rates by offering financial incentives to stay in school, and *not* to engage in crime – clearly reflect this securitized social assistance approach. As in other Latin American countries, where at-risk marginalized youth are considered to be a potential source of violence and insecurity due to the likeliness of them joining gangs or criminal insurgents such as drug trafficking organizations (Hochmüller and Müller 2016), the Mexico City programme involves 'extensive surveillance over the city's residence and regular visits from social workers to residents' houses' as 'efforts to reduce crime and violence by increasing the presence of the state in the lives of individuals' (Luccisano and Macdonald 2013).

Far from being impartial initiatives to empower local residents – in particular in marginalized neighbourhoods – such programmes merge the governance of security and welfare 'by regulating communities and "deserving" individuals' by appealing to an idea of 'active citizenship that focuses explicitly on enabling targeted populations' to contribute to their own security according to governance priorities defined by responsibilizing bureaucracies in the name of the neoliberal governing of poverty as a potential source of instability and insecurity (Schild 2015: 10).

The overall result of this development is that the PRD's efforts to demonstrate that it can 'secure' Mexico City has made the party adopt punitive policies within the realm of law enforcement and welfare that, in the end, are 'similar to those of [Mexican president] Calderón [PAN], even under a socialized agenda, promoting high-impact operations, coercion, surveillance, and incarceration' (Valenzuela Aguilar 2013: 29).

Conclusion

This chapter analysed how the intersection of the urbanization of neoliberalism, the democratization of local politics and the consolidation of PRD rule contributed to a growing penalization of urban marginality, and the related transformation of Mexico City into a punitive urban city. Not only does this city show a remarkable continuity with its authoritarian predecessor, through the punitive governing of urban marginality, it also increasingly excludes, through criminalization and penalization, the most marginalized segments of the urban population, in particular those labouring in the city's expanding informal – and criminalized – economy, whose lives the local democratization process was expected to improve. However, these processes are not confined to the formal/institutional realm. As the next chapter will demonstrate, by turning to the resilience of political clientelism, the consequences of these developments can also be observed within the realm of informal politics. In this regard, the next chapter demonstrates how, in a context in which the economic survival strategies of those at the urban margins are increasingly criminalized and subject to penalizing politics, those who rely on the informal economy for their socio-economic reproduction have become increasingly dependent upon the political protection offered by patrons with good connections to politicians and bureaucrats who can influence local law enforcement in their favour. Thereby, the transformation of Mexico City into a punitive city strengthened rather than undermined the existence of informal political structures by increasing the dependence of those on society's margins upon informal means of protection and safety from criminalizing state politics.

CHAPTER 2

Neoliberal insecurities
and resilient clientelism

Nearly a decade after the CCE published its strategy paper, mentioned in Chapter 1, in which the local business community decried the decline of Mexico City's historic centre because of an existing 'culture of illegality' and a 'new mafia power that draws on old and new corporatist and clientelistic vices' (CCE/CESPEDES 2001: 11), the Secretariat of Public Security of the Federal District (SSPDF) distributed a leaflet on citizen participation in security matters, which ended with the following disclaimer:

> This programme is of public character. It is not conveyed nor promoted by any political party and its resources come from the taxes paid by all taxpayers. It is forbidden to use this programme for political and electoral goals, for pecuniary rewards or any other purposes different from those established in the programme. Anyone that will make an improper use of the programme's resources in the Federal District, will be sanctioned according to the respective law and from the responsible authority. (SSPDF 2009)

Both documents, CCE's strategy report and the SSPDF leaflet, are related to a phenomenon that will be at the centre of the analysis of the present chapter: the resilience of political clientelism in Mexico City, its expansion into the realm of security provision and its resulting contribution to the punitive turn in local politics. The subsequent analysis will demonstrate that in contemporary Mexico City, the securitization of urban space, which accompanied the neoliberalization of the local economy, created a context in which the informal economic survival strategies of those at the urban margins are increasingly criminalized and targeted by punitive politics. Thereby large segments of the city population working in the informal economy have become dependent upon the political protection offered by patrons with good connections to politicians and bureaucrats who can influence local law enforcement in their favour. This process, as the chapter furthermore illustrates, is embedded in a more general remaking of clientelist practices during the local democratization process and their expansion into the realm of security governance. The latter development is related to the fact that in a political environment marked by a precarious security situation that makes security a top priority for the local electorate, security-related service delivery through clientelist channels serves as an important political resource for politicians interested in building up political support.

In analysing these processes, the present chapter moves beyond the formal top-down processes behind the transformation of Mexico City into a punitive city. In looking beyond and behind official discourses and formal practices, the chapter provides insights into the everyday manifestations of the punitive turn in local politics. The analysis demonstrates how the urbanization of neoliberalism, the repercussions of the local democratization process and the political top-down and bottom-up responses to urban insecurity expanded the punitive turn to the realm of informal politics. Unpacking these processes is not only important for understanding the informal privatization and decentralization of security provision and coercion in contemporary Mexico City and how these processes feed into the growing punitiveness of the urban everyday. Such an analysis is also essential for sensitizing readers to the fact that democracy and, in particular, neoliberalism, which are often portrayed as powerful macrostructural phenomena that are at odds with clientelism (e.g. Roberts 2014: 97; but see Hilgers 2012), far from bringing an end to clientelism reinforce the latter, ultimately undermining the publicness of local security governance. This, in a self-reinforcing cycle, makes urban citizens, in particular urban marginals, increasingly dependent upon privatized protection provided through clientelistic channels.

The chapter starts with a historical contextualization of political clientelism in the city in order to better assess continuity and change regarding the role of informal politics in local urban governance. It moves on to the more recent expansion of clientelist relations into the realm of security governance, the related conversion of public security into means of *private* protection and coercion, as well as the growing dependence of those at urban society's margins on *political* protection from the punitive consequences following from the securitization of urban space discussed in the previous chapter.

Clientelism in Mexico City: then and now

A central pillar of the political system that emerged out of the Mexican Revolution of 1917 has been the thorough penetration of social and political relations by clientelist practices, considered as 'the giving of material resources as a quid pro quo for political support' (Stokes 2007: 667). The type of clientelism that stood at the heart of the Mexican political system during seventy-one years of PRI one-party rule has been described as 'authoritarian clientelism', that is a form of 'political subordination in exchange for material rewards' in which 'imbalanced bargaining relations require the enduring political subordination of clients and are reinforced by the threat of coercion' (Fox 1994: 154).

Authoritarian patron–client exchange penetrated the entire political architecture of the post-revolutionary state (Magaloni 2006), including capital city politics in Mexico City (Cornelius 1975; Eckstein 1998). However, clientelist relations do not just exist 'out there'. They have to be crafted, produced and reproduced by political means. The founding episode that inscribed political clientelism into the heart of Mexico City politics was the abolishment of the municipal governance structure of Mexico City in 1928 by President Álvaro Obregón. This move placed Mexico City's governance under the direct authority of the Mexican president and his appointed mayor (Davis 1994: 61), thereby creating a particular dense entanglement of local and national politics that defined urban governance in the city for most of the twentieth century:

From 1928 to 1997, the Federal District had no independent rights and became a centralized, managed entity under federal power. The mayor, or *regente*, was hand-picked by the president and the 16 *delegaciones* or precincts had *delegados* hand-picked by the mayor, without a city council to offer the necessary supervision or framework of accountability. The mayors ranged from political heavyweights to close friends of the president, and prior to 1988 not a single one of them was a Mexico City native. The political structure was organized around issues of political and social control, caving in only when necessary and managing dissent in the same fashion as the PRI ruled the country as a whole. (Castillo 2008: 184)

In Mexico City's urban politics under PRI rule, the central role of authoritarian clientelism in 'managing' capital city politics was most visible in the way the PRI machine organized political support. The basic exchange relation was rather simple: by offering personalized informal access to urban infrastructure, public services or jobs, the PRI expected electoral support and other demonstrations of political loyalty from the beneficiaries of these services. Local residents participated in these relations, because it was impossible to get access to public resources and state bureaucracies on an impersonal, formal rational-legal basis (Grindle 1977). Under such conditions, the PRI's 'punishment regime', which threatened to exclude oppositional actors (politicians as well as voters) from the clientelist spoil system, was largely efficient in securing high levels of electoral turnout (Magaloni 2006).

But PRI-style authoritarian clientelism in Mexico City also had an institutional dimension. What can be called the PRI's particular brand of 'bureaucratic clientelism' (see Müller 2013a) in Mexico City included the distribution of patronage resources throughout the administrative apparatus and the PRI's party organizations. As employment opportunities and career options in the city administration were not merit-based but largely dependent upon political calculations, personal loyalty and membership in informal patronage networks, or *camarillas*, the upward mobility of local politicians and bureaucrats was ultimately dependent upon their capacity to create informal linkages with organized civil society actors and to convert these relations into means for enhancing their own political capital (Cross 1998: chapter 3).

In turn, these agreements provided organized civil society groups – and their leaders – with privileged access to state agents and resources in exchange for supporting local politicians, bureaucrats and/or the PRI as such, thereby entangling the institutional and societal dimensions of PRI-style authoritarian clientelism in the city. While the underlying 'tactic and irregular agreements with city officials' (Cross 1998) also included the distribution of employment opportunities to middle class subjects, clientelist relations in Mexico City mostly involved the marginalized segments of the local population, like informal street vendors or land squatters, a fact that reflects the widely established correlation between poverty and the prevalence of political clientelism (e.g. Stokes 2007: 661–663) or, to be more precise, 'the political uses of poverty' (Fernández Muñoz 2008). Through the incorporation of those at urban society's margins into clientelism-based urban governance, political support for the PRI regime was traded for the provision of infrastructure, the formalization of squatter settlements, lax law enforcement or the toleration of informal, frequently illegal, economic activities (Cornelius 1975; Cross 1998).

Such clientelist exchanges were mediated by political brokers who became the informally recognized representatives of neighbourhood-level collective interests vis-à-vis local bureaucrats and politicians. As in other Latin American cities, bureaucrats and politicians, in turn, found in marginalized urban communities 'the cheapest possible source of political support' (Fischer 2014: 22):

[I]n exchange for a water spigot, or a little protection from an avaricious landlord, or a willingness to block enforcement of a whole range of laws banning settlement, a politician could gain votes from thousands, none of whom could legitimately demand expensive urban services. At a local level, those able to organize a community and deliver its gratitude in votes became newly critical cogs in the urban political machine, often using the experience to launch political careers. (Fischer 2014: 22)

The institutionalization of these informal patron–client relations, in fact a veritable informal institution-making process grounded in patron–client exchanges, in the guise of what Bartra called 'structures of mediation', in and through which political support was traded for particularistic rewards, contributed decisively to the stability of the post-revolutionary political system under PRI hegemony (Bartra 1999: 27).

Although joining the game of political clientelism might have been a rational decision for the recipients of such forms of particularistic rewards, and a functional (and functioning) prerequisite for the exercise of political power under PRI rule, it would be misleading to conclude that political clientelism was all-pervasive and successful in preventing the emergence of oppositional political movements or the open contestation of PRI rule in Mexico City. In fact, neither the material inducements authoritarian clientelism could offer, nor the informal social control exercised by political strongmen, or *caciques*, who 'often accompanied by armed guards, dominated many poor communities, collecting "donations," ostensibly for bribes and other costs of doing business with the government' (Schlefer 2008: 37) and exercised 'informal police powers' for crushing local opposition to PRI rule (and their own power) (Cornelius 1975: 146), really pacified Mexico City's political landscape.

Not only was Mexico City the earliest bastion of the political opposition in Mexico. In addition to this, as political clientelism rests upon the permanent promise and delivery of material inducements, the economic crises of the 1980s, the resulting arrival of neoliberal austerity measures and the related dismantling of the PRI state (Aitken et al. 1996) seriously undermined the capacity to fulfil such promises, leading to a growing defection of urban poor voters to Cuauthémoc Cárdenas and his Frente Democrático Nacional (National Democratic Front, FDN) in the 1988 presidential elections. Many of these voters came from the expanding informal urban service sector (such as taxi drivers, domestic employees, low-level bureaucrats, etcetera), thereby representing diverse interests that the PRI was no longer capable of successfully organizing and rallying behind its presidential candidate (Magaloni 2006: 186–187).

With the transformation of the FDN into the PRD in 1989, the broad and heterogeneous political coalition that stood behind the FDN became institutionalized and organized itself around the figure of Cárdenas. More than anything else, this process reflected a compromise between 'an intellectual elite' and 'representatives of the popular classes [*representantes populares*] who had no deeper [political] training and emerged from clientelistic networks [*las filas clientelares*]' (Baena Paz and Saavedra Andrade 2004: 217). This compromise deeply affected the internal workings of power inside the PRD as well as the party's relation to the local electorate. As Hilgers has argued in this regard, it was the emergence of Cuauhtémoc Cárdenas as the predominant political leader within the party and his decision to beat the PRI in the electoral realm as soon as possible, which inscribed clientelist practices into the PRD's internal workings of power:

> As a result of Cárdenas's desire to oust the PRI from power, to do so in the electoral arena, and to do it as soon as possible, the PRD focused resources on elections. The resources, including time, that would have been necessary for institutionalizing party rules and regulations to ensure internal cohesion and democratic procedures were not available. As a result, leadership and alliances were personalized, and factions battled for power. When the PRD began to win local and state governments, these tendencies spilled into its administration and played out as clientelistic relationships with citizens. (Hilgers 2008: 124)

In light of this scenario, it is not surprising that when, following constitutional changes, in 1997, the residents of Mexico City could for the first time since 1928 elect the local mayor, Cárdenas won the electoral race and established the PRD's hold over Mexico City, personalism, factionalism and political clientelism continued to thrive in the nation's capital. Bartra described the resulting political structure as a 'dense clientelistic network', through which the distribution of economic and social assistance, public investments as well as the legalization of illegal practices – such as land occupations – are informally negotiated between the Mexico City government and the representatives of the marginalized segments of the local population.

According to him, 'this structure constitutes a pyramid of mediations which runs through the borough administrations and on whose top stands the mayor of Mexico City' (Bartra 2007: 67).

Internal party structures and practices of the PRD thus played a crucial role in reproducing political clientelism in post-authoritarian Mexico City. Yet, a second factor that is key in explaining the local resilience of clientelism stems from the embeddedness of the local democratization process within the larger neoliberal transformation of Mexico's political and economic environment. In Mexico City, this process, as shown in detail in Chapters 1 and 3, contributed to growing economic polarization and impoverishment of large segments of the urban population – most visible in the growth of the informal economy throughout the last decades – as a consequence of the Global City-oriented urban development model, the city's related deepening integration into neoliberal globalization processes and the resulting securitization of urban space. Under such conditions, it becomes apparent that the growing number of un- and underemployed segments of the local population, in order to guarantee their socio-economic reproduction 'must choose between going without much-needed resources and using personal relationships with local politicians, operators and social leaders to obtain housing, services and work' (Hilgers 2009). To put it another way, the negative socio-economic consequences of neoliberalism in the city strengthen the dependence of those at society's margins on clientelist service delivery, thereby pushing them to the status of second-class citizens (on this issue, see Koonings and Kruijt 2007), whose access to public goods does not depend upon their status as legally entitled citizens, but rather on personalized, and politicized, access to people with access to these goods. The resilience of clientelism in the city thus has both an economic (neoliberalism) and political (democratization) basis.

The following transcript from an interview with a resident of a marginalized Mexico City neighbourhood offers a paradigmatic description of how such clientelist exchanges take place and how the PRD uses the vulnerability of urban marginals to enhance its local support base:

And then, what they do is, for example, to go to the neighbourhoods [*venir a las colonias*]. They pay some guys [*chavos*] who go and tell the people that they're coming from the PRD. And that they are coming so that people can tell them what they need. 'Tell me what you want because we can solve this'. 'You need money', or money through the cards they distribute for the elderly and the single mothers and similar things. 'You want education, you want work?'. And then they tell you 'Give your signature on this form from the governor [sic!]'. And because the people believe them, because it's like 'Yes, yes, it's certain that they will give me….', therefore they pull out a sheet with the PRD logo which is a request form for becoming a PRD member. And then they tell the people: 'You want all of this, but you have to sign so that the governor can give you these things […].' So what they do is to collect [signatures] and go the party and say 'We have 5000 people'. Then they go to the social housing projects [*unidades habitacionales*] and say 'I'll give you paint, I'll give you this but you'll have to vote that day. And you must vote for the borough mayor [*el señor delegado*] […] because it is him who gives you all of this. If you will vote for him he will continue giving you [these things].' This is what they do and in this case it is similar to what the PRI has done, even if they're no longer in power, but it's the same thing. (quoted in Müller 2012c: 191, modified translation)

The point the interviewee makes about the role of local *delegados* points towards another contribution the local democratization process made to the ongoing presence of political clientelism in the city. Since 2000, the local population for a three-year term elects the heads of the sixteen Mexico City boroughs, or *delegaciones*. This decentralization of political power, at first sight, seems to enhance the power of local residents and their impact on political-decision making. Under the given structural conditions mentioned above – notably the legacy of clientelism inside the PRD and the growing dependence of urban marginals on clientelistic networks as a consequence of the negative socio-economic impact of the urbanization of neoliberalism – political decentralization, instead of empowering local residents, adds another layer of patron–client relations to the local universe of informal politics. This is, in particular, because political decentralization provides local politicians with additional resources that allow them to establish clientelist exchange relations with their voters (Cobilt Cruz 2008; see also Vite Pérez 2001: 216–217).

While the democratization of Mexico City politics did not bring an end to political clientelism, the political repercussions of the local democratization processes, nonetheless, substantially transformed the exercise of political power through clientelist practices and the way clientelism operates in the city. When compared to PRI's authoritarian clientelism, which was an essentially imbalanced bargaining relation that was reinforced and supported by the always given threat of coercion and repression (Fox 1994: 153), the democratization of Mexico City politics *tendentially* empowered clients at the expense of their patrons.

One decisive factor contributing to this development is the reduction of the level of coercion that underpins these relations. This is related to the fact that because of the PRD's own historical experience with extra-legal coercion, the use of force and coercion 'never formed an accepted element of clientelism in the party [the PRD]' (Hilgers 2009: 55). In this regard, clientelist relations that are used for coercing residents to vote for local politicians – a situation that has been observed, for instance, in urban Brazil where drug traffickers and militias are engaged in such more coercive forms of clientelist exchanges (Arias 2006; Moreira Alves and Evanson 2011)* – are the exception rather than the rule in Mexico City. The underlying reluctance of the PRD to insert outright use of force into clientelist exchanges in Mexico City might also explain the absence of clientelist forms of collective violence, based on party-broker-police linkages that have been documented by Auyero in his analysis of the 2001 food riots in Argentina (Auyero 2004: 77–86; 2007). While this, as will be shown below, should not be read as if clientelism in contemporary Mexico City lost its 'stick', the overall decrease in coercion in local patron–client exchanges is nonetheless noteworthy and central to the tendential empowerment of clients vis-à-vis their patrons as a consequence of the local democratization process.

Another factor contributing to this outcome is the growing dependence of political patrons upon the outcomes of formal democratic practices and competition. One important aspect that has to be kept in

---

* For a detailed analysis of the methods used by drug traffickers to control the 'secret' vote, see Perlman (2010: 206).

mind in this regard relates to the fact that the interpersonal exchanges involved in patron–client relations are, as pointed out by Hilgers, deeply affected by the political environment in which they operate:

> [T]he dynamics of PE [clientelistic personal exchanges] change according to the [political] context, and, in particular, the intensification of political competition and the democratic opening enhance the advantages of PEs for their consumers, rendering these exchanges more participatory and generating more accountability on the part of the providers (commanditaires). (Hilgers 2011: 140).

In addition to this, Hilgers' research on the PRD in Mexico City has provided ample evidence of how these changes were further stimulated by the effective diversification and pluralization of the Mexican party system. This is the case because in Mexico City's democratic political context, patrons 'must compete vigorously for clients who can now choose among candidates from various parties'. In this competitive context, 'clients have significant direct negotiation powers because patrons make their bids in the client's presence and must outperform each other. Patrons are easily identifiable, easily held accountable and the rules of the game are clear' (Hilgers 2009: 70). This more competitive form of political clientelism particularly affects the PRD because 'fierce electoral "democratic" competition between the different PRD currents reinforced existing informal political practices on the ground' (Denissen 2009).

These developments are embedded in the wider dismantling of the corporatist structures that were essential for the workings of clientelism under PRI rule. In fact, Mexico's corporatist arrangements that emerged during the post-revolutionary state formation process deeply inscribed a form of 'corporatist clientelism'* into the routine exercise of power during the decades of one-party rule. Based on the integration of the Confederación de Trabajadores de México (Confederation of Mexican Workers, CTM), the Confederación Nacional Campesina (National Peasant Confederation, CNC) and the Confederación

---

* On 'corporatist clientelism', see Ansell and Mitchell (2010).

Nacional de Organizaciones Populares (National Confederation of Popular Organizations, CNOP) into the PRI, Mexican state–society relations were mediated and negotiated through the party's corporatist pillars and clientelist goods provision, as the following quote sums up in a paradigmatic way:

> This corporatist apparatus depended in part on the informal patron-client relationships that pervaded much of Mexican society. For example, the ubiquitous street-vendors in Mexico City paid a local boss to occupy space, as if public sidewalks were for rent, while the boss kept the authorities and rival vendors at bay. Mafiosi-like *caciques*, often accompanied by armed guards, dominated many poor communities, collecting 'donations,' ostensibly for bribes and other costs of doing business with the government. For all their inflated commissions, they did secure benefits such as land titles, water services or street grading from politicians. Those politicians in turn vying with each other to prove their effectiveness to higher authorities required the caciques to produce masses of supporters at rallies, prevent social unrest, and avoid building alliances with other communities. (Schlefer 2008: 37)

Although it would be wrong to assume that with the end of PRI rule Mexican corporatism is dead,[*] in the case of Mexico City, the PRD attacked and undermined basic pillars of the PRI's corporatist structures, which further improved the negotiation power of clients vis-à-vis their patrons. A telling example in this regard is the case of informal street commerce that, as the previous quote correctly suggests, was probably the most visible manifestation of corporatist clientelism in Mexico City under PRI rule.[†]

During the PRD's rise to power in Mexico City, the party was able to modify existing legislation and established that every person capable of organizing ten people could establish a civil association (*asocia-*

---

[*] For a good overview of the development of Mexican corporatism, see Zapata Schaffeld (2004).

[†] Most street vendor organizations were affiliated with the PRI through the CNOP.

ción civil). This was accompanied by a political strategy that aimed at encouraging the formation of civil associations by political functionaries and people close to the PRD who were working for borough administrations and in the realm of informal street commerce. The overall goal of this strategy was to break up the monopoly of PRI-affiliated street vendor organizations and their leaders by pluralizing the political organizational landscape related to street commerce. This strategy was particularly successful in the area of Mexico City's historic centre, where the PRI's corporatist monopoly over street vendor organizations was strongest. The resulting fragmentation of the previously existing corporatist structures represented a threat for established leaders of street vendor organizations. To counter this threat, many leaders chose to expand the spectrum of clientelist service delivery beyond the usual guarantee of a vending place for members of their organizations. To this end, they added welfare-related services into the repertoire of membership benefits. In doing so, they hoped to buy the loyalty of their members and to impede their desertion to other leaders (and their organizations) (Zaremberg 2010: 154–155). This response clearly reflects how the PRD's fragmentation strategy enhanced the power of the members of street vendor organizations (clients) at the expense of their patrons (leaders) by offering the former some kind of exit option out of authoritarian organizational structures.

Similar developments can also be observed with regards to the relationship between politicians and the leaders of street vendor organizations. This relationship, according to Zaremberg, has always been determined by the leaders' interest in using the politicians' access to bureaucrats in the borough administration to solve problems stemming from conflicts between the borough administration and leaders. In exchange for this commitment, leaders promise the support and loyalty of their members to politicians willing to solve their problems. However, in an increasingly competitive electoral context and a pluralized party landscape, leaders use political actors mostly on the basis of cost–benefit rationales, irrespective of the politicians' party affiliation (Zaremberg 2010: 154). To put it in other words, in contrast to the years of one-party rule, in Mexico City's democratic political environment, party membership and affiliation has become a secondary political factor in determining the relationship between leaders and politicians, giving the former more flexibility and making it easier for them to switch from one politician incapable of solving the leaders' problems to another, more promising political patron, thereby putting pressure on patrons to offer and comply with 'good deals'.

Despite all these changes related to the democratization of local politics, it is beyond doubt that political clientelism in contemporary Mexico City continues to be an overly imbalanced bargaining tool. However, and when compared to the decades of PRI rule, the balance of power has shifted more in favour of the clients, making patron–client exchanges less coercive and more flexible. Long ago, James C. Scott argued that patron–client relations are situated along a continuum ranging from overly coercive relations towards those characterized by high levels of 'free choice', in which clients are able to manage their problems mostly without the active help of a patron. Scott mentions four factors determining where a given patron–client relation is placed on this continuum: the level of coercion involved in the relation, the client's access to goods and/or services desired by the patron, the availability of competing patrons, as well as the client's chances of managing his or her problems without the patron's help. The more beneficial a particular configuration of these factors is for the client, the more the underlying power relation changes in his or her favour (Scott 1972: 93–94).

Applying this argument to the case of Mexico City, it is obvious that, as a consequence of the democratization of local politics, all dimensions except the last (the client's chances of solving his or her problems without a patron) have been altered in favour of political clients: politicians now, more than ever, depend upon the clients' votes; the level of (formal and informal) coercion that sustained PRI-clientelism has been substantially reduced; and clients now can (and do) choose among different and competing patrons (from different parties as well as from within the PRD).

In addition to these transformations, another important aspect in which contemporary clientelism in Mexico City differs from the authoritarian clientelism that characterized capital city politics during the years of PRI rule consists in a more general diversification of clientelist services and their expansion into the realm of security governance. It is this expansion that links the resilience of clientelism discussed in this section to the more general transformation of Mexico City into a punitive city.

Clientelism and (in)security

The fact that security provision has become an important currency within contemporary patron–client exchanges in Mexico City first of all reflects efforts by local residents to search for means of protection outside – largely inefficient, if not absent – officially sanctioned channels of security provision in an increasingly insecure urban environment – and that brokers and politicians have been receptive to these demands. As in contemporary Mexico City, crime, fear and insecurity are some of the most relevant issues on the urban political agenda (see Chapter 1), and, as shown in the previous section, the democratization of Mexico City politics did not bring an end to political clientelism, it seems only logical that citizens accustomed to and socialized under political clientelism search for informal solutions to the growing insecurity problems from below.

This bottom-up demand for more informally provided protection, on the other hand, is accompanied by a top-down response because local politicians, brokers and political bosses also discovered that offering security and protection through clientelist channels has become a (politically) attractive business (Denissen 2009: 420). In other words, local politicians have recognized the growing demand for alternative and informal solutions to local insecurity problems, and they are more than willing to serve them, in exchange for political support, through clientelist practices.

The clientelist provision of protection is, in many cases, determined by party politics and the relationships between different factions of the PRD in the boroughs, as well as between different party factions in the boroughs and the Mexico City PRD government. The latter uses access to public resources, including security-related resources, in order to distribute them for building up or strengthening its own local support base. As one resident from a marginalized Mexico City neighbourhood described it:

[T]hese practices of the political parties. Yes, they exist everywhere. For example the PRD. The governor of the Federal

District, Marcelo Ebrard, he has no support base here. At least he is not a person who during his political career has worked with the popular organizations, with the *colonias*, so he doesn't have many people that support him. But now that he is the head of the government of the Federal District he can use public resources for his interests.

In such a context, the responsiveness of public institutions is perceived as something that does not depend upon impartial, impersonal legal-rational conduct, but on membership in clientelist networks, contacts, preferences, calculations and negotiations, leading to the selective distribution of security resources and privileging people with good connections to political bosses, bureaucrats and/or politicians, as the following transcript from another interview with a local resident illustrates:

> Well, this is a PRD neighbourhood, which is a left-wing party. So, many local politicians here are members of the local parliament. There are many people working for them as well, and because they are close to the PRD and because the government of the Federal District belongs to the PRD, there are obvious preferences. Here, they have always maintained these privileged relations, the tradition of having good connections to politicians or the police. […] But the normal people of course don't have this kind of personal access. They must always establish a personal relationship with someone and thereby strengthen [*reforzar*] this person's political career.

As the preceding interview passage indicates, the access to clientelist networks that permits privileged access to informal forms of security and protection is uneven and hierarchical. Not everyone possesses the political and/or social capital necessary for a direct and unmediated relationship with local politicians. Therefore, the participation of many residents in these relations and the opportunities for them to gain access to these informal processes of the distribution of security resources are in many cases mediated through local political brokers. Such behaviour is tolerated by the local authorities, as it represents a crucial feature of the practices of negotiations or *gestiones* that are central to informal politics in Mexico City: in exchange for the delivery of services to local residents, the latter offer political support to people capable of providing these services. This relationship is frequently not a direct one, but mediated through local brokers or intermediaries. Their power is based on political capital derived from their capacity to mobilize people. This in turn enables them to function as informal spokespersons of local-level collective interests and to represent these interests to state authorities. This capacity gives such brokers a privileged access to state personnel and resources – including security – that can be appropriated to a certain degree for their private and political purposes (Hilgers 2008: 137).

In this regard, local residents frequently referred to the *jefe/jefa de manzana*, whose privileged access to local politicians and the *delegación* was perceived as not only facilitating the local residents' access to public resources (including security and protection), but also, as indicated in the preceding interview passage, strengthening the local brokers' political capital:

What measures did you take in order to confront the security problems?
Well… the surveillance… There was one woman, the *jefa de manzana*. […] There is this person related to our block, who is in charge of all the problems. And later, this woman, [because of her], well they've sent more, well, they've put more security, they've assigned more patrol cars.

[…]

So would you say that this system of the jefes de manzana works?
Yes, it's like a support system, because you go to her and she goes to the *delegación*. It is through her that many things have been accomplished here, in this part of the *colonia*.

And does she do it without receiving any gifts or the like?
No, no, no. Nothing. On the contrary, it's good for her, because she has support. If one day you want to help her in some case,

> you go and you give her your vote, your signature. And she says [to the local authorities]: 'You see, I have gotten together 100 signatures from different people whom I have helped, and now they are helping me.' That's how it works with her.

While such forms of clientelism-based security provision can be called reactive, as they emerge from the bottom-up demands of local residents, brokers and local politicians also engage in more top-down protection and security practices. Such efforts, for instance, include the organization of informal security guards (*vigilantes*) that police certain areas, in particular in marginalized neighbourhoods, in exchange for political support (and frequently money). The following quote from an interview with a resident in a marginalized Mexico City neighbourhood offers insights into the related dynamics:

> They [the vigilantes] were created when Arturo Sánchez [this name is a pseudonym] was president [sic!] of the borough. He called it a proposal for vigilance. At the beginning there were about 30 of them and they were accepted because they were more constant in their surveillance [than the regular police], but what was not good is when they became bodyguards of the low-ranking politicians [*pequeños políticos*].

While some residents feel uncomfortable with such informal and often politicized security arrangements, this is mostly because the involved security providers frequently tend to charge local residents for their services. While this is sometimes perceived as threatening, it should be highlighted that, as argued in the previous section, such informal arrangements are not generally used for coercing residents to vote for local politicians.

Although the basic deal involved in such forms of security-related patron–client exchanges in Mexico City is that the receiving people are expected to offer political support to their service and protection providing patrons and brokers, it is important to stress that political support not only takes the form of classic vote-buying. While the issue of (coercive or non-coercive) vote-buying, which dominates much of the related literature, is undeniably relevant, demonstrating political support, in exchange for service provision, implies more quotidian practices. In fact, elections are only one element within the involved patron–client exchanges and the routine party politics that underpin the everyday workings of political clientelism through which brokers solve their clients' everyday problems and in doing so 'accumulate political capital that helps them advance in the political field' (Auyero 2007: 55–71). Such political capital accumulation is inseparable from public performances that demonstrate that the broker is capable of mobilizing a loyal political following, for instance through the latter's participation in political rallies, political festivities and/ or, most frequently, by putting their signatures on a list compiled by their broker that he or she can show to politicians as evidence of his/ her support base. These signs of support are used by brokers and/or politicians for enhancing their standing and position either inside the faction-ridden PRD or, in case of an independent broker,* by offering support to competing PRD politicians – in exchange for access to jobs, public services and/or money. It is through these more quotidian activities rather than through direct, and due to the secret ballot hard to control, electoral means that resources, including security and protection, are provided and (mediated) political power is accumulated through patron–client exchanges, as the interview quote above on the *jefa de manzana* illustrates.

But this interview passage also illustrates another important aspect behind the expansion of clientelism into the realm of security provision. The *jefes/jefas de manzana* were intermediary local neighbourhood representatives that have been created by the PRI as a central element within the city's clientelist governance structure. The institution was finally abolished by the PRD with the enactment of the Ley de Participación Ciudadana (Citizen Participation Law) in 1997 and replaced by the so-called neighbourhood or citizen committees. The fact that interview partners from marginalized communities frequently continue to refer to the representatives of the committees as *jefes de manzana* can be seen as clear evidence of the more or less uninterrupted continuity of clientelist relations inside intermediary

---

* On the growing independence of local brokers from political parties in contemporary Mexico, see Zárate Hernández (2005).

administrative institutions of citizen participation in contemporary Mexico City.

In fact, as the general persistence of political clientelism in contemporary Mexico City is, to a large extent, related to the institutional redesign that accompanied the democratization of local urban governance (see above), the expansion of clientelist exchanges to the realm of security provision can also be explained by the emergence of an institutional 'opportunity structure' that is the direct product of the democratization of local politics.

Reflecting the double-edged sword of fiscal and political decentralization in Mexico (Cornelius 1999: 12), this development is facilitated by Mexico City's growing budget throughout the last decade, as well as the expansion of a variety of comparatively decentralized citizen participation programmes within the framework of the Citizen Participation Law. Both developments provide a permanent flow of resources – to a substantial degree financed by federal fiscal transfers that increased from 5,9 million Pesos in 2000 to 12,6 million Pesos in 2006* – that are largely independent of immediate electoral results, but which enable political entrepreneurs at the centres of resource distribution to become political patrons by providing jobs and access to public security in return for publicly visible political support – facilitated by a highly arbitrary nature of security spending (see Müller 2013a: 555-558).

Within the faction-ridden PRD, this political support is the most important resource for political upward mobility and survival, which is most visible in the fact that 'candidates are courted purely on a calculation of who heads the best clientelist networks' (Hilgers 2009: 152). It has been the expansion of decisively local government programmes that facilitated this *tendential* de-coupling of patron–client exchanges from immediate electoral results – although a good neighbourhood broker is still able to deliver votes – and for converting them into important means through which inner-party factional conflicts are fought out and power relations modified.

In fact, much of the protection-related patron–client exchanges take place through this recent expansion of citizen participation programmes

---

* www.finanzas.df.gob.mx/fiscal/docs/EstadisticasFiscales.pdf.

within the realm of security governance and the related general make-over of bureaucratic clientelism inside the local police forces under PRD rule (Müller 2013a, 2013b). For example, as shown elsewhere in greater detail, the related practices include the clientelist appropriation of community policing programmes, such as the so-called *policía de barrio* (neighbourhood police) project (Müller 2010a; see also Tello 2012), and the related accountability institutions, the abovementioned neighbourhood committees. The latter are legally entitled to articulate the security interests of the respective communities and they have an annual budget of about 500.000 Pesos at their disposal for local crime prevention activities. This converts them into highly attractive 'booty' for local brokers and politicians that manage to capture the committees and channel the related resources to their followers in exchange for political support. The following transcript from an interview with a former director of a citizen participation programme for crime prevention in Mexico City is indicative of these processes:

> You know that the *Ley de Participación Ciudadana por el D.F.* created mechanisms for [citizen] participation. Like, for instance, the neighbourhood committees, but they have not been re-elected for 9 years. In fact, the idea of political representation, everything that has something to do with citizen participation is devoid of any content [*es muy vacía*]. [...] This means that you don't have any community representation, any citizen representation that serves as an interlocutor with the borough administration. There is no strategy for linking the community to the borough administration. For us, this was the main issue. The part of the community always develops slowly, because inside the borough administrations there are many internal fights about monopolizing access to the community. [...] The problem is that there is no secure basis regarding what things the community asked for from the borough administration. And later on, the borough administrations set up the requests and defined how and where to buy these things. There was lot of corruption. This is a fact. Lots of corruption from the authorities. At this stage it became clear to me that the requests made by the neighbours had not much to do with the results. It had

nothing to do with what the people had requested. In the end the solution from the authorities was more or less arbitrary. They bought what served them to make the deal. [...] In fact, there has been much corruption in the subcommittees. [...] Members of the subcommittees had the *policía de barrio* basically under their command. They converted the policemen into private vigilance.

Such forms of private vigilance are largely arranged through individual negotiations between local residents and political brokers, such as politicians, local political bosses or bureaucrats who convert their privileged access to public security resources into an informal coercive resource that allows people with access to clientelist networks for using the latter, as one interviewee put it, to 'threaten [...] and scare' one's 'opponents'. Providing informal access to coercion, in turn, is an important means for furthering a broker's own political career, as the following passage from an interview with a local resident in a marginalized Mexico City neighbourhood illustrates:

Here we have a recurrent big problem. [...] There are people who can say 'I have a friend who is a police commander' and they pay him some money [*pagan una lana*] and they'll send you a police car with judicial police agents and arrest person X and there's impunity. But in general, the majority of the people don't have such access. They always need to relate to someone whose political career they're going to support.

Such practices contribute to the emergence of violent patron–client exchanges in which 'violence brokers' (Koonings and Kruijt 2007: 14), local residents, but also state actors, negotiate deals regarding the delivery of votes, policy implementation and more general provision of political support. Thus, the conversion of public security resources into 'private vigilance' not only takes the form of physical protection and the provision of safety. In many cases, the clientelist appropriation of public security resources also serves highly coercive forms of local/private conflict resolution, the enforcing of one's own interests, or as a means for protecting illegal businesses, including drug-trafficking, from law enforcement (Müller 2012a: 332–337, 2012c: 186-188).

In this regard, the expansion of clientelism into the realm of security governance adds an informal dimension to the punitive turn in Mexico City politics. It disperses and de-centres public violence by allowing actors endowed with substantial political, economic and/or symbolic capital to privatize public security resources for particularistic interests. While this has been a constant feature of Mexico City policing and its overdetermination by clientelist practices (e.g. Davis 2010; Müller 2013b), the abovementioned expansion of neighbourhood-level citizen participation programmes in combination with the recent transformations of clientelism in the city, exacerbate these processes and give them a new quality. In a perverse way, these developments democratized, dispersed and further decentred violence in Mexico City by facilitating informal access to coercive state resources outside and beyond previously existing monopolistic PRI party structures that kept the clientelist dispersion of public violence somehow under control.

However, the most visible expression of the relationship between the resilience of clientelism and the transformation of Mexico City into a punitive city is the securitization of urban space targeting, in particular, the city's informal economy. While the regulation of informal commerce through clientelistic means, as shown in the previous section, has been a constant feature of PRI rule in the city, the rise of the PRD reinforced these processes through the securitization of urban space and the related enacting of new laws aimed at safeguarding the neoliberal urban renewal efforts in downtown Mexico City (see Chapter 1).

This outcome, as shown elsewhere in more detail (Müller 2016a: 236-238), provides ample evidence for the at first sight counterintuitive fact that far from dismantling clientelism through a deepening of the rule of law, the expansion and application of the rule of law has substantially contributed to the resilience of clientelism and the punitive turn in local politics, thereby transforming the rule of law into the *rule through law* (see introduction). In Mexico City, as argued in Chapter 1, the securitization of urban space translates into a growing legal productivity of the PRD governments. This resulted in the enactment of several laws that explicitly target undesired manifestations of urban marginality and economic informality – such as street vending, squeegee cleaning or public drinking – in order to attract foreign investment for real-estate development in the area of the historic centre with the goal of enhancing the city's position in global neoliberal urban competition. As the police have become the main institution in charge of the so-called rescue project in downtown Mexico City, the related penalization of poverty increasingly exposes those at society's margins who are forced into working in the informal economy to the threat of punitive and often violent policing practices. While, as argued above, historically the informal economy has been deeply embedded in patron–client structures that traded legal non-enforcement for political loyalty to the PRI, the PRD's neoliberal turn in combination with the expansion of the city's informal economy in recent years substantially modified this context. This is the case because the PRD's interest in safeguarding urban renewal has increasingly raised the costs for the affected people to bargain over the non-enforcement of laws and to engage in rule-bending practices with local patrons and/or bureaucrats. In this regard, punitive measures such as the introduction of detention quotas, referred to in Chapter 1, as well as the related financial reward and promotion system for police officers complying with their quota, has raised the financial stakes for the urban poor to bribe their way out. As a result of this, 'the very survival of these people [working in the informal economy] now depends in full on the discretion of police officials' (Campesi 2010: 460).

The growing number of people depending on clientelist protection from punitive law enforcement represents a political challenge as well as an opportunity for PRD politicians (Hilgers 2008; 2009). On the one hand, politicians are confronted with the necessity and public pressures to regulate the city's informal economy. On the other hand, they also face the pressure from organized informal actors making a living in the informal economy. The PRD's response to this situation has been the selective enforcement of certain regulatory and legal standards, and, at the same time, the crafting of informal alliances between different PRD factions and organized informal actors, 'using the group's electoral strength to increase their own bargaining power in negotiations for positions and policy direction inside the party' (Hilgers 2008: 134). The protective spill-over effect of such negotiations for people connected to organized informal actors is evident and clearly reflected in statements like the following: 'Yes, there are many people who are close to the PRD here, and I, who belong to the PRD, well the party gives me... well, it protects me.' And as long as such protection also implies being protected from neoliberal lawfare tools and punitive policing, joining clientelist exchanges continues to be an important element within local residents' everyday survival strategies in Mexico City's contemporary political and insecurity context. This not only further contributes to the resilience of clientelism in the city, it also contributes to the punitiveness of informal politics. As those outside clientelist networks are basically left without protection from punitive law enforcement, they become the main victims of the punitive makeover of urban governance in the city, which is clearly reflected in the socio-economic composition of the local prison population, described in Chapter 1. In this regard, while the straightforward and directly politically motivated coercion that underpinned PRI-style authoritarian clientelism might have disappeared in the city, the securitization of urban space added a new layer of coercion to the local universe of patron–client exchanges, one that is increasingly felt by those who have been pushed to the margins of urban society in neoliberal Mexico City.

Conclusion

This chapter has demonstrated that far from being a phenomenon exclusive to the seventy-one years of authoritarian PRI politics, political clientelism is alive and well in Mexico City's contemporary democratic environment. It was shown that the urbanization of neoliberalism, the repercussions of the local democratization process and the political top-down and bottom-up responses to urban insecurity expanded the punitive turn to the realm of informal politics. As the democratization of Mexico City politics was accompanied by and embedded in a growing deterioration of the local security situation, in a mutually reinforcing process, bottom-up demands for protection met with the discovery of the political gains local politicians and political brokers could derive from offering informal protection in exchange for political support. The overall result of this has been the diversification of the spectrum of clientelist services, as well as the increasing expansion of clientelism into the realm of security governance and the broader punitive transformation of urban politics.

In this regard, the evidence presented in this chapter calls for a sceptical appraisal of the frequently assumed incompatibility of clientelism and democracy. In fact, the findings demonstrate that the democratization of local politics itself was an important causal factor behind the inclusion of security provision into the local universe of clientelist exchanges. While this situation might provide short-term benefits to both politicians facing the pressures of democratic electoral competition, as well as citizens in search of additional protection, the long-term consequences of such arrangements are more than problematic. They contribute to the resilience of clientelism as an inherently imbalanced bargaining relationship that reinforces processes of punitive exclusion and marginalization in the realm of informal politics. However, as the next chapter will demonstrate, by turning to bottom-up responses towards neoliberal penalization targeting the informal economy in two neighbourhoods in downtown Mexico City, informal politics are also the domain in which the punitive turn in contemporary Mexico City is contested and negotiated in and through multiple forms of resistance and contestation from below.

CHAPTER 3

Lawfare and resistance
at the new urban frontier

Throughout Latin America, neoliberalism's 'going urban' has converted many of the region's cities into 'strategic targets and proving grounds for an increasingly broad range of neoliberal policy experiments, institutional innovations and political projects' (Peck et al. 2009: 65). Through this process, Latin American cities are transformed into veritable 'incubators for, and generative nodes within, the reproduction of neoliberalism as a "living" institutional regime' (ibid.). As shown in detail in Chapter 1, a central element of the Latin American urbanization of neoliberalism has been a securitization of urban space that elevated security and urban (dis)order concerns regarding the proper use, design and (re)ordering of urban space to one of the most important policy concerns of the local administrations (see also Becker and Müller 2013: 79). This securitization process is inseparable from 'the universalisation of forms of public administration' (Atkinson and Bridge 2005: 2), in particular within the realm of legal regulations and policing. This is the case because urban policy makers throughout the world have largely accepted that the presentation of a city as a safe place for international investment increasingly determines a city's performance in inter-urban competition. Therefore, the expulsion of urban undesirables, like homeless people or those working in informal and increasingly criminalized economies, is seen as 'vital for the success of the postindustrial city and to its business community' (Belina and

Helms 2003: 1845–1847). As a result of this, neoliberal policy-makers have increasingly resorted to the implementation of urban policies designed to guarantee the 'freedom' of the market 'by law, authority, force, and, *in extremis*, by violence' (Harvey 2000: 179) in order to clean 'the built environment and the streets from the physical and human detritus wrought by economic deregulation and welfare retrenchment so as to make the city over into a pleasant site of and for bourgeois consumption' (Wacquant 2008c: 199) – and investment.

As shown in detail in Chapter 1, this development contributed substantially to the transformation of Mexico City into a punitive city. While Chapter 1 offered an in-depth discussion of the punitive turn in local politics at the macro level, the present chapter follows up on this by zooming in on the unfolding of this process in two sites of Mexico City's historic downtown, the area most affected by the securitization of urban space. Most of the related studies on urban revanchism in neoliberal Latin America tend to focus on elite actors (political and/or economic) and how their interests in safeguarding the urbanization of neoliberalism lead to the implementation of repressive and punitive policing practices. While this is undeniably important, this focus, however, often tends to portray non-elite actors as passive subjects (see also Koonings and Kruijt 2015a: 18). In focusing on the reactions of those affected by neoliberal urban renewal projects, this chapter takes a closer look at these developments and how they unfold at the micro level. It focuses on two sites of what, following Neil Smith's work on urban revanchism (see introduction), can be termed Mexico City's 'new urban frontier' (Smith 1996). The frontier metaphor calls attention to the fact that many proponents of neoliberal urban renewal projects treat marginalized inner-city populations 'as a natural element of their physical surroundings' and designate the spaces in which they live as 'not yet socially inhabited', thereby rationalizing and legitimizing 'a process of conquest' (Smith 1996: xiv–xv).

In offering an in-depth assessment of the attempts to conquer the Merced neighbourhood – the city's main red light district – and Tepito – Mexico City's crime hot spot – as well as the related policing- and lawfare-backed efforts of imposing neoliberal visions of urban order, this chapter highlights how local actors confronted with the arrival of neoliberalism in their neighbourhoods apply and engage in multiple forms of resistance and contestation. These practices range from the exercise of symbolic and physical violence, to informal bargaining processes through clientelist channels, to 'hidden transcripts' (Scott 1990) in the guise of symbolic mimicry, the spreading of rumours, or the creation of subaltern counter-publics. While many of these efforts are successful in impeding the unmediated unfolding and expansion of neoliberal urban renewal projects in downtown Mexico City, this chapter also reveals that in general only those neighbourhood actors with sufficient political, symbolic and economic capital benefit from this outcome, while those at the margins of the punitive city increasingly face the penalizing consequences of the securitization of urban space.

Urban renaissance in the old Merced area*

For a closer approximation as to how the above-mentioned processes of securitization and penalization concretely materialize in downtown Mexico City, we shall take a look at the efforts of upgrading the area of La Merced neighbourhood in the southeastern part of the historic centre, Mexico City's traditional red-light district. Three aspects make the neighbourhood particularly interesting for assessing the way urban renewal processes are negotiated and contested from below. First, the area is of crucial importance for the expansion of the urban renewal project of the administration of Marcelo Ebrard (2006–2012). Under Ebrard, the spatial scope of the renewal effort extended beyond the historically better-off areas in the western parts of the historic centre between Alameda Park and the Zócalo – where expensive hotels, offices, fancy boutiques and jewellery shops can be found – to the more popular and run-down areas in the southeast of Perimeter A. Second, as about 40 per cent of the heritage protected buildings in downtown Mexico City are located in the Merced area, it can be considered to be an attractive site for the development of heritage tourism, which, as mentioned in Chapter 1, is a cornerstone of the local Global City strategy. Third, the neighbourhood is a paradigmatic example of a

---

* I am thankful for Anne Becker's permission to include interview material from her fieldwork in this section.

territory where urban renewal and neoliberal globalization confront the presence of powerful networks of 'other', and from the vantage point of the proponents of neoliberal globalization 'illiberal' globalization processes and economic networks that are often linked to informal and criminalized economies of those at urban society's margins, and which resist the renewal project by competing for the control and use of urban space (Davis 2008). In the Merced area, these networks are in particular linked to street vending, human and drug trafficking, as well as prostitution, especially of minors.

To briefly describe the neighbourhood, the Merced is located southeast of the Zócalo on the former frontier between the Spanish colonial centre and the indigenous boroughs. For centuries, it has been the commercial and transshipment centre of the city. Until 1982, the Merced market – which covered up to fifty-three blocks – had been the city's largest wholesale grocery and food market. Street vending, a long-standing activity in the Merced, and textile manufacturing also characterized the neighbourhood, which became a 'popular commercial corridor that linked Tepito with the Merced market' (PPDUCH 2000: 27). Yet, the construction of a new central market in the eastern part of the city in 1982, the earthquake of 1985, declining investments of real estate proprietors, the increasing informal transformation of residential space into warehouses, and the recurrent economic crises contributed to the social and economic decline of the area and converted this part of the historic centre into the 'last space of survival of the most vulnerable groups of urban society (indigenous migrants, homeless people, disabled or mentally ill persons, single mothers, street children, old people)' (Coulomb 2000: 531). Notwithstanding these developments, and in contrast to a massive depopulation of the more affluent parts of the historical centre since the 1970s, the old Merced neighbourhood still maintains a residential character. Today, its residents belong to the most marginalized and poorest segments of the city population, with high percentages of indigenous migrants who often squat in abandoned buildings that lack basic infrastructure (PPDUCH 2000: 36–38, 42). For centuries the area has also been the main red-light district of Mexico City. Today, networks of human trafficking and forced prostitution operate in the area, which according to the Attorney General's Office is a multi-billion dollar business and linked to drug and arms smuggling in Mexico. According to a grass-roots sex worker organization, these mafia networks manage about thirty illegal brothels in the area and constitute a permanent source of violence and slavery-like exploitation. In order to keep their business running, it is estimated that these illegal entrepreneurs pay some 450,000 US$ a month to the police and municipal authorities (*La Jornada* 2009). These illegal actors informally closed – and literally appropriated – public streets in order to convert them into 'catwalks' [*pasarelas*] (*La Jornada* 2008). Although no exact number exists, street prostitution in the Merced has increased significantly since the 1990s, and it is estimated that between 2,000 and 3,500 sex workers offer their services here (*Revista Contralínea* 2008).

These interrelated developments contributed to an urban environment that was perceived as a serious obstacle for the recent urban renewal efforts of the Ebrard administration. In order to transform the area into a more inviting neighbourhood, in 2007 street vendors were expelled from the area. Street prostitution is still widespread, but sex workers complain about abuse, police harassment, and their removal from the upgraded areas of the neighbourhood (*El Universal* 2009). Several run-down heritage protected buildings have been – illegally – demolished by the local authorities in order to construct market halls for ex-street vendors. In order to protect these efforts, a securitization of the neighbourhood, inspired by the Giuliani report, discussed at length in Chapter 1, was initiated: New police stations opened in the area and in 2007, the precinct mayor announced his intention 'to not only improve the cityscape and police interventions in terms of crime prevention, but also to eradicate prostitution' (*Revista Contralínea* 2008). In May 2008, the local Tourist Secretary announced a government plan for the area and openly acknowledged the investor-oriented focus of the plan. According to him, the government was pursuing the 'rescue' of the Merced in order to 'attract private investors' and to 'dignify and transform the area into a focal point of investment in tourism, real estate and commercial development, together with neighbours and formal merchants'. The stated goal was to provide conditions in which the neighbourhood's 'buildings and churches that date back from the 16th to the 19th century can be admired once again' and to 'incorporate the Merced into the city in a more visible, productive and dignified way, making it an enjoyable place'. In order to pursue this goal, the government was to recuperate public space as well as real estate property used as warehouses, restructure the Merced market, eradicate prostitution and street vending, combat drug trade and reconstruct community ties in the area (*La Jornada* 2008).

In 2008, the restructuring of the built environment of the eastern part of the Perimeter A was initiated: Urban infrastructure was renewed, public spaces were redesigned, pavements renewed, rubbish bins and CCTV cameras installed, and facades repainted. A central concern of this transformation of urban space is the promotion of heritage tourism. The area is part of a pedestrian 'cultural corridor' (*corredor cultural alhóndiga*) that links many historic sites in the city. In interviews, local authorities stated that they were preparing a tourist guide and tourist signposting systems for the area in the hope that federal and private investments to rehabilitate real estate would follow and that new cafés, restaurants and heritage tourism-related services would soon begin to operate in the area. However, according to an employee from the Tourism Secretariat of the Federal District, the newly created Authority for the Historic Centre (Autoridad del Centro Histórico) would like to begin immediately with the tourist promotion of the Merced, but his office vehemently opposes this plan and insists that it is 'still necessary to clean up the area before you can send a tourist there'. According to him, the continued presence of street prostitution, homeless people and criminal activities 'are factors that constrain tourism' and 'have to be removed first'. Consequently, the local tourist office 'will insist on limiting the effort to the touristy parts of the Perimeter A and leave the other areas for a second stage because we do recommend that other government institutions responsible for the removal of *these things* [*sic*!] [sex workers, homeless people, delinquents, loose cables, signposts] must act in the first place'. To understand the ongoing presence of these 'obstacles' to urban renewal, we have to take an even closer look at the implementation of the renewal effort at the street level.

If we examine the actual implementation of the local urban renewal processes in the Merced area, it becomes apparent that these developments are not smooth top-down processes. Rather, they are challenged, contested and mediated by several factors, among which the most important seem to be the presence of illegal actors and the existence of informal structures and practices of negotiation linking these local actors with state authorities (see also Crossa 2009). Government authorities are well aware of the fragile and contested nature of the project and the resulting negotiations over urban space in the neighbourhood. The latter result in particular from efforts of illegal actors to undermine and to obstruct activities related to the expansion of the renewal effort. For instance, as the head of the real estate development department of the Historic Centre Trust (FCH) explained, construction work in the proximity of the *pasarelas* and illegal brothels has not been easy: 'We had to make huge efforts to renew the streets, materials and tools were frequently stolen, construction workers were knocked down and engineers assaulted.' Aware of its powerful competitors, the promoters of urban renewal seek to confront their illegal rivals along a territorial and property-oriented logic, aiming at the physical displacement of criminality and the expansion of a 'frontier of legality', frequently leading to what the FCH interviewee called the 'cockroach effect':

We started with these public works to make these persons aware that legality is approaching. We installed street lightning. These are signs and signals of what is developing here and of what [activities] will not be able to develop here any longer and what has to move to some other place. You will tell me: 'Well, they will move to the other side of Circunvalación [a highway dividing the Perimeter A and B] and that there are more prostitutes in the Venustiano Carranza borough and that this is the cockroach effect'. Well, that's right. [...] It is a very hard, a very difficult, reality. We attacked the Hotel Universo [confiscated in March 2009]. This is where, I do not say that this is the only place, but it is a very large space where terrible networks, terrible persons operated. We try to act against them, demonstrating our firm commitment. These initiatives are meant to make them understand that they either change business or go somewhere else.

As this quote illustrates in a paradigmatic way, beyond the official 'law and order' rhetoric, many security efforts and police interventions that accompany the neoliberal upgrading of the area are most of all symbolic acts of communication through which local authorities, residents and illegal actors (re)negotiate the shape and unfolding of the urban renewal process. They are not about law enforcement proper. Rather, such activities can be considered as a symbolic show of force that aims at intimidating illegal competitors over the use of urban space in the area and to pressure them 'to change their business or go somewhere else'. In this regard, it is of little surprise that a sex workers' rights organizations criticized the activities of the local authorities as mere symbolic interventions (*La Jornada* 2009). Such processes contribute to an apparent spatial selectivity of the urban renewal effort in the area, reflecting the informal power of illegal actors to challenge the official vision of the future of the neighbourhood and to successfully negotiate over the use of urban space. As a result of this, the *pasarelas* continue to exist next to renewed streets and rehabilitated buildings, as do most of the illegal brothels. Moreover, historically important streets on the southern edge of the Merced, such as parts of Roldán street and Santo Tomás street, have been left out of the renewal process. In the mental map of local residents, however, these are the most unsafe areas of the neighbourhood, 'where you know that it is very dangerous for everybody to go there and look, they did not renew, they did not touch these streets, only a small part. I did not understand why they left out all the rest. [...] Those areas where the brothels and drugs are most strongly present have not been touched'.

Within the local urban renewal process, such negotiation processes not only involve illegal actors. Members of the neighbourhood's informal economy also participate in these processes, in particular as one of the central goals of the local government has been to liberate the streets of the Merced from informal street vendors. As mentioned above, until 2007 the streets of the old Merced were covered with street vendors. According to official discourse, the 'liberation' of the streets of the Perimeter A from street vending has been an exemplary success: It is represented as the outcome of a negotiated solution accepted by 15,000 vendors, who according to the agreement were to be relocated in market halls. Yet, street vendors working in the neighbourhood have a different opinion on this subject. In their eyes, the physical relocation only benefited their leaders and, to a lesser degree, the most affluent vendors who were relocated in well-located market halls. In interviews they complained that the government still tolerates leaders imposing their own system of fees for occupying space as well as for related 'services' in the market halls, as the following interview passage demonstrates:

When López Obrador removed us from the streets he offered us economic help, supposedly with the idea to calm us down. [...] It was a bit more than 5,000 Pesos each, split into three payments, every check around 2,000 Pesos. But [name of the leader] kept 600 Peso of each check for herself of all the thousands and thousands of street vendors. If you refused to give her the money, she would take away your place, she would take away your work space. So what do you do? The government knew of all of this. [...] And if you are a merchant and the market hall does not pay out for you, finally you will abandon it and look for another place, and they [the leaders] will stay with the market halls, although these spaces have been created for us. These spaces are a big lie that the government used to get us off the streets. We are the most affected because we do not have a space to work if you do not have the money to pay the fees the leaders charge you.

A member of the Subsecretario de Programas Delegacionales y Reordenamiento de la Vía Pública (Sub-Secretariat for Precinct Programs and the Restructuring of the Public Space) in charge of the negotiation confirmed the existence of these practices. As he explained, 'the market halls have been handed over to the leaders. Nothing else was possible, since we could not negotiate with and treat individually tens of thousands of street vendors'. As a result, he went on to explain, 'we cannot do anything about it when leaders charge vendors money in the halls, but we tell street vendors that the leaders have no right to do that and that they should make a formal complaint at the public ministry'. To put it in other terms, in order to achieve its goal of removing the undesired presence of informal economic activities from the streets of the Merced (as well as of other parts of downtown Mexico City), the local administration tolerates the continuation of frequently highly exploitative and coercive leader–street vendor relations in exchange for the leaders' commitment to get their people off the streets, thereby strengthening the leaders' image of people who deliver.

Those street vendors unwilling to do so frequently decide to sell their good as so-called *toreros*. *Torear* means to sell goods as 'traveling vendors' (*toreros*) on the streets – equipped only with a small blanket or plastic bags which can be picked up and hidden as soon as the police approach. However, according to street vendors, *toreo* is a very exhausting, precarious and risky activity. As a *torero* explained, the police patrol sometimes passes by every fifteen minutes. This not only increases the possibility of being arrested, it also threatens to make street vending impossible. Moreover, as many street vendors stated in interviews, even after the negotiated removal of the street vendors, local leaders maintain control over *their* streets and continue to charge daily fees for *torear*. The member of the Sub-Secretary, introduced above, openly admitted that 'although leaders and government struck a political agreement, leaders still give the opportunity for *toreo*, and many police and municipal inspectors of public space are still willing to turn a blind eye to the *toreros* and claim their bribe'. In fact, and this is another manifestation of the negotiation processes that shape the selectivity of the local urban renewal process, in some parts of the Perimeter A, such as the Merced, *toreo* is tolerated by the police. As the following passage, taken from an interview with a street vendor, demonstrates in a paradigmatic way, local police officers not only frequently abuse their authority, they are also more than willing to negotiate over legal enforcement measures, and the presence of *toreros* on the streets of the neighbourhood, in exchange for monetary incentives:

For example, I put a blanket on the pavement, I lay out some blouses and I watch out, I mean, I feel I can never fall asleep. I always look from where they [the policemen] might arrive: 'Yes, feel free to have a look, mister, yes, take a look'. You respond and you watch out again, you cannot be distracted because suddenly they arrive to get you, because they do. [...] The day they caught me, they pulled me out of a shop, although they are not allowed to trespass a private establishment. I mean, the government violates the law as it pleases.

[...] They got me into a police car. [...] The only thing I told him was: 'You know what, don't touch me'. Because they take you or your merchandise and steal it. I said to him: 'No, don't touch me, you've already won'. I said to him: 'I get in the car myself', and I picked up my merchandise and I got in the car myself, because the people who resist are torn or even beaten, like animals. And they take you to the civic judges. This time I managed to get off the car, I mean, I made a deal with them because it was Sunday. It's said that Sunday's judge is very bitchy, so I said to them: 'Don't be mean, let me get off.' I told him: 'Look, it's late.' It was six o'clock. 'At what time will they get me on the list?' Because you have to wait for your turn, one by one they write down your name, what you sell, where you sell, where they caught you, all this, and your entrance hour is the time you are registered, the 24 hours count from that time onwards in case you do not pay the fine. If you pay the fine it also depends on the judge. They say that some judges charge you less: 'What do you sell?' 'I just sell hair clips, I earn very little.' 'How much?' 'Only 50 Pesos a day.' So your fine will be less, let's say, 100 Peso. Some judges are very good people. If you manage to arrange such an amount, you get out, but if they charge you 500, you won't. Who can pay 500 Peso if what you have in your pocket is hardly enough to cover your expenses?

And how was the deal that day?
Well, I paid them 100 Peso and they let me go.

As this example clearly demonstrates, another important factor – in addition to situational aspects, such as the day and time of the arrest as well as the potential value of the detained person – which represents an additional obstacle for a sustainable breakthrough of the local urban renewal effort, stems directly from the institution which should be expected to serve as the ultimate guarantor of its success: the police. Far from being a simple instrument in the hands of the local government, the local police forces have historically been characterized by a high degree of autonomy (Müller 2012c; Martínez de Murguía 1999). This autonomy facilitated the emergence of an extra-legal culture inside the local police, which found its expression in the existence of corruption and patronage networks that pervade the entire police apparatus and that affect and frequently over-determine the everyday practices of the local forces and the entire apparatus of the administration of justice. As an ex-member of the local police apparatus explained in an interview, practically everyone who comes into conflict with the law in Mexico City can negotiate – most of all through bribery – the outcome of this conflict. In his words, 'The law does not cost 10 Pesos, but for just 100, you can buy your liberty'. As long as these informal structures persist inside the local police apparatus, we should expect that the contribution of the local police forces to the success of the renewal efforts at the local and street level is highly contested and ultimately a matter of negotiation, the result of which cannot be determined beforehand. This will be further illustrated in the next section, which will present an analysis of different forms of resistance and contestation aimed at confronting the growing criminalization of the informal economy of the Tepito neighbourhood and related efforts of integrating the area in the 'repressive gentrification' (Campesi 2010) process unfolding in downtown Mexico City.

Changing patterns of illegal entrepreneurship and political regulation in Tepito

At least since the nineteenth-century Tepito neighbourhood, located in close proximity to the presidential palace and the *Zócalo*, the main plaza of Mexico City, has occupied a central place in the local urban imagination, which is closely related to illegal activities and crime. As Garza observed in this regard:

> Tepito, whose original name was Mecamalinco, dated from colonial times. By the 1880s the neighborhood had shed its indigenous name but had retained the poverty, transforming it into a dangerous zone in the eyes of metropolitan observers. Fattened by thousands of rural migrants, who either lived in flimsy dwellings or moved into tenement buildings, Tepito acquired an exotic reputation and an aura of criminality even

though many of its residents were mainly working-class artisans. It still possesses this notoriety today. (Garza 2007: 18)

In fact, until the middle of the twentieth century, Tepito was most of all a neighbourhood where the city's lower classes purchased cheap, used, repaired/recycled, stolen contraband goods (Marek 2010: 533). Most of this merchandise was sold on informal street markets. Research has extensively documented how the informality and illegality of most of Tepito's economy served as a means for political negotiation and mediation between the leaders of street vendor organizations, the city administration and the PRI; negotiations in and through which selective law enforcement and the toleration of illegality were traded for political support and loyalty (and, of course, bribes) (e.g. Alba Vega 2010; Castro Nieto 1990; Cross 1998; Eckstein 1988; Müller 2012c: 144–148).

> In Tepito, the open sale of contraband became an important source of employment during the second half of the century, following an expansion of street commerce in general. Its ability was made possible by the clientelistic relations that existed between the neighborhood merchant associations and the PRI. The importance of these relations was directly linked to the street merchant's vulnerability to inspectors and policemen: in the absence of specific regulations, all street sales were, in one way or another, illegal. Organizations worked as 'mafias' that sold protection. In exchange, authorities benefited from, among other things, the mobilization of *tepiteños* in PRI demonstrations. (Piccato 2007: 73)

The forms of illegal entrepreneurship that sustained and resulted from these political relations, and the related 'tactic and irregular agreements with city officials, notwithstanding the official claims of illegality' (Cross 1998: 16), changed dramatically during the neoliberal turn in Mexico during the 1980s and 1990s, in particular after Mexico signed the General Agreement on Tariffs and Trade (GATT) in 1986 and liberalized its economic relations with the US. While most of the contraband consumer goods that were sold in Tepito – and that dominated its economy during the 1960s and 1970s – came from the US, the liberalization of trans-border trade that followed Mexico's GATT entry 'unconsciously destroyed the smuggling industry on the Northern border' (Sadler 2000: 174). As previously hard-to-find consumer goods now were basically available for everyone in Mexico, classic consumer goods-centred contraband activities became a non-profitable economic dead-end. Following Mexico's economic crisis and another round of trade liberalization that resulted from the country joining the North American Free Trade Agreement (NAFTA) in 1994, classic contraband commerce that focused on electronic consumer goods was increasingly replaced by the emergence of 'new illegalities' (Aguiar 2012) in the form of pirated software, DVDs, CDs, clothes, but also by trafficking in drugs and weapons (Davis and Ruiz de Teresa 2013: 118–120). In addition to this, Tepito-based contraband networks increasingly expanded to Asia, in particular China and South Korea, leading to both a growing presence of Asian entrepreneurs in the neighbourhood as well as the emergence of transnational supply chains for pirated products/related raw materials like CD-Rs. The growing importance of transnational trade networks, linking Tepito with Asia, for instance, is reflected in the fact that one of the most important organizations for informal street vendors in Tepito, the Metropolitan Front of Popular Organizations (Frente Metropolitano de Organizaciones Populares, FMOP) has recently opened an office in the Northern Chinese city of Yiwu to improve its transnational trade relations (*El Universal* 2010). While such processes point towards a growing diversification and pluralization of economic actors/interests in Tepito, they also introduced new (transnational) illegal actors and activities into the local economy. As one related report observed:

> South Korean merchants have become an important commercial force in the neighborhood, owning some 300 of the 700 warehouses in Tepito and commanding perhaps one-third of the market's sales. South Korean organized crime groups have established a racket to control Asian vendors in the area and have spurred the growth of a thriving gun-running business in the market, as well as trade in counterfeit apparel and accessories from China. (Treverton et al. 2009: 168)

In addition to such developments, the growing presence of illegal entrepreneurs engaged in the trafficking of drugs and weapons, while far from being dominant within Tepito's illegal political economy, was accompanied by increasing violence within the neighbourhood. Within the context of rising security problems since the mid-1990s, these overall changes of the internal composition of Tepito's illegal economy under neoliberalism converted the neighbourhood, once more, into the territorial symbolization of urban crime and violence – a process that has been exacerbated by transnational security discourses and their vernacularization (see Chapters 1 and 4) – clearly reflected in apocalyptic accounts like the following:

> Tepito is the Casbah of Mexico City, shadowy and serpentine, its back alleys vanishing into sinister, dead-ends. Here underground tunnels lead to thieves' dens, and clandestine warehouses are stuffed with stolen goods. You do not want to be caught out after dark in this 'barrio bravo' when it crackles with gunfire. So far in 2003, 32 bullet-riddled corpses have turned up on these mean streets in a battle for control over the flourishing drug trade. Tepito is Mexico City's hottest drug 'plaza', the city's pirate goods capital and, as even a casual observer might conclude from the number of gun deaths here, a world class weapons bazaar. (Ross 2003: 18)

Containing such negative international and national publicity has been a central concern of the local PRD governments and their interest, discussed in detail in Chapter 1, in implementing a neoliberal Global City-centred urban development model that aims at attracting international investors, in particular within the realm of real-estate development in the area of downtown Mexico City. During this process, the neighbourhood itself has increasingly become the object of neoliberal urban renewal efforts, as the following quote, describing the meeting of a colleague with Víctor, a local political activist of the United Movement of the Tepito Neighborhood (Movimiento Unido del Barrio de Tepito, MUBT), illustrates:

> 'A small contribution against the general disinformation' the scraggy man smiled. A couple of cardboards displayed print-outs

from the website of the government of Mexico City. Three-dimensional models of monumental glass palaces and broad boulevards, along-side company logos: the Mexican telecommunication giant Telmex, the department chain Sanborns, the supermarket chain Walmart, the retailer of consumer electronics, the mobile phone company Nokia, the sport department store Martí and a couple of other leaders in the field. Newspaper articles from la Jornada and El Universal complement the collage. Above this is written, with a thick marker: 'Tepito es mi barrio' [Tepito is my neighbourhood]. Víctor grabs two wooden boxes. 'Don't bother to write down the web address. The drawings are no longer online. By now, the city government prefers to present its development plans for Tepito only to selected persons.' (quoted in Brock 2008: 213)

When considering the central role of informal politics in local urban governance, it comes as little surprise that despite the undeniable criminalization of the neighbourhood's economy, as in the old Merced area, the concrete unfolding of these processes is mediated and negotiated by informal politics. Activities by people like Víctor represent one observable practice through which local actors try to contest the advancement of securitizing urban renewal in their neighbourhood.

Following Fraser (1990), such practices can be defined as efforts of creating 'subaltern counterpublics'. These are 'parallel discursive arenas where members of subordinated social groups invent and circulate counterdiscourses to formulate oppositional interpretations of their identities, interests, and needs' (Fraser 1990: 67). As Fraser illustrates with regards to the feminist movement in the US, subaltern counterpublics have manifold manifestations, including, for example, publications, lecture series, local meeting places, or research centres (ibid.: 67). In the case of Tepito, however, subaltern counterpublics largely centre around the activities of street vendor organizations or neighbourhood organizations like MUBT that feel threatened by the envisioned neoliberal upgrading of the area and the related securitization process. While not publishing journals or organizing lecture series, the manifestations of these counterpublics take, for instance, the form of information booths on local markets. Here activists inform residents, vendors and customers about the consequences of state activities aimed at containing the neighbourhood's informal economy and present alternative development ideas. Subaltern counterpublics in Tepito also include meetings organized by different neighbourhood and street-vendor organizations in which their members – and residents in general – are informed about the planned rolling-out of neoliberalism in Tepito, discuss possible responses and organize the printing and distribution of leaflets or, more commonly, posters for the circulation of counter-discourses.

While there are no lecture series, Tepito also has more institutionalized arenas of alternative and resistant knowledge production. The most famous outlet in this regard is the Centro de Estudios Tepiteños (Centre for Tepito Studies), founded in 1984 and located at 56 Heroes de Granaditas on Eje 1 Norte. The centre operates its own website (www.barriodetepito.com.mx/), which welcomes its visitors with the following message: 'The Tepito neighbourhood exists because it quietly resists like a coil spring, smart as a match' (*Siendo barrio Tepito existe porque resiste quieto cómo un resorte, listo como un cerillo*). Among other things, the website offers a virtual tour through the neighbourhood. It provides 'information about its history as well as critical comments on political and economic actions directed against its residents and economic structures that counters official portrayals of the neighbourhood. When considering the fact, that, according to the site meter on the Centro's web page (6 May 2011) already some 89,219 internet users have consulted barriodetepito. com.mx, it should be apparent that this information has a wide circulation whose scope is even enhanced by more traditional forms of knowledge diffusion in the guise of brochures and leaflets produced by the Centro. This information is not just distributed among residents, merchants and ordinary visitors to the area; another target audience of this counterpublic institution consists in local and international academics, as well as journalists, who frequently visit the Centro, as it provides an important and useful first entry point to the neighbourhood. Through such contacts, academics and journalists become important multiplicators of the Centro's counter-hegemonic discourse. Even if we assume that journalistic and academic self-reflexivity might protect them from an uncritical reproduction of the

Centro's discourses and agenda, the fact that this audience adds a further, national and international, dimension to such forms of subaltern counterpublic knowledge production should be obvious. This is also clearly reflected in the presence of leading figures of the Centro, such as Alfonso Hernández, Tepito's self-proclaimed chronicler (and the Centro's founder), in academic conferences and journals (e.g. Hernández 2008).

In addition to such activities related to counterpublics, another element within the repertoire of the 'politics of the governed' (Chatterjee 2004) in Tepito, as in the case of La Merced, consists in the strategic and symbolic use of violence against state authorities, in particular the police. In this regard, it should be kept in mind that since the new millennium, Tepito has witnessed an increasing number of large-scale police raids, involving hundreds of highly armed local and federal police forces. In addition to the interest in safeguarding the urban renaissance project in the historic centre and the urban renewal-related 'recuperation of public spaces' in Tepito itself, such efforts are also related to the militarized rhetoric of contemporary Mexican law enforcement and its multiple wars against drugs and piracy. When considering that the International Intellectual Copyright Alliance (IIPA) in all of its related reports and recommendations on Mexico presents Tepito as the most notorious place of the violation of intellectual property rights in the country, it is of little surprise that the neighbourhood has increasingly become the object of related police actions, the so-called *tepitazos*. These actions are nearly always accompanied by violent clashes between police and hundreds of *tepiteños* (Piccato 2005).

Such confrontations can be analysed as another element pertaining to the repertoire of the local politics of the governed in which violence constitutes an important element of the political negotiation processes regarding securitizing urban politics in downtown Mexico City. In fact, for many local actors such police raids and the resulting confrontations are interpreted as a symbolic show of force that prepares the terrain for subsequent informal political negotiations between the informal/illegal economy and the local authorities regarding the informal spatio-political regulation of Tepito's economy (and the extent of bribes) (see also Müller 2012c: 147).

However, the actual and symbolic use of violence that underpins these negotiation processes is mostly successful when the involved actors are embedded in political patron–client networks. I already argued above that under PRI rule, patron–client relations and the 'tactic and irregular agreements with city officials, notwithstanding the official claims of illegality' were the single most important factor behind the consolidation and reproduction of illegal entrepreneurship in Tepito. These relations continue to dominate the local governments' relations to the urban poor and the informal sector in general, often trading political loyalty and bribes in return for the non-enforcement of existing laws (Chapter 2). What changed under PRD rule is that the aforementioned diversification of economic actors and interests, as well as the factionalism inside the PRD, has substantially decentralized the highly centralized forms of patron–client-based negotiations that shaped Tepito's political economy under PRI rule. In the new democratic urban environment, such clientelist negotiations are more open to contestation from below. Under these circumstances, resorting to collective forms of spectacular violence, I would argue, has become an important means through which organized actors of Tepito's informal economy accumulate political capital that provides their organizations with additional political resources – in the guise of a 'threat potential' – that can be traded as a currency in informal negotiations with the local government.

In this regard, the fear of violent retribution expressed by local police authorities after one of the most spectacular police raids in the area – the expropriation and demolishing of a housing complex (*vecindad*) located at Tenochtitlán (street) 40 in February 2007, involving about 600 police officers and special units (*El Universal* 2007b) – should be interpreted along those lines.

On 16 February 2007, the official gazette of Mexico City, *Gaceta Oficial del Distrito Federal*, published an expropriation decree for the abovementioned *vecindad*. The expropriation was necessary, it was argued, because in these buildings people 'engage in diverse forms of delinquency, such as the sale of drugs, stolen goods, the reproduction and sale of video recorded or audio material, which represents a risk for the security of the area' (*se realicen diversas actividades delictivas tales como venta de estupefacientes al menudeo, artículos robados, reproducción y venta de material video grabado o de audio, lo que ocasiona un riesgo para la seguridad en la zona*) (Gaceta Oficial del Distrito Federal 2007: 3). Following this decree, the previously mentioned police action took place, leading to the expulsion of about forty families, the arrest of about a dozen people, and the demolishing of the buildings. According to official statements, about sixty apartments had been used for illegal video reproduction and drug trafficking. Police records also documented 'departments with double bulletproof doors, multiple high-security locks and electronic alarm systems, secondary entries through the ceiling, ad hoc security rooms on the roofs, and false walls that revealed hidden rooms and tunnels hidden behind furniture and mirrors' (Davis and Ruiz de Teresa 2013: 122).

When I visited the area in June 2007, the buildings were already completely demolished and the terrain was shielded off from the surrounding streets by a metal fence and protected by a detachment of police officers. After the expropriation, newspaper reports pointed towards responses from within the neighbourhood along the lines of the politics of the governed discussed above: organized mobilization and negotiations with public authorities. For example, a march of about 200 people to the city government was organized and headed by María Rosete Sánchez, the leader of one of the most powerful street vendor organizations, in order to negotiate with local authorities over this issue and impede further expropriations in the area (*La Jornada* 2007a), an effort which, in light of the absence of further expropriations in the neighbourhood, seems to have been successful.

But in addition to such practices, in my visits to the area after the expropriation, I also came across other responses from the local population, like the circulation of narratives about the 'true story' behind the expropriation of 'El 40' or '*la fortaleza*' (the fortress). These narratives portrayed the expropriation as resulting from the greedy economic and shady personal interests of the government. For instance, one story about the expropriation argued that this was only the first in a row of other expropriations through which people in the government of Mexico City would plan to invest their private money in the neighbourhood in order to gain economic benefits from the related redeveloping of these spaces for themselves. Another story explained the expropriation with a personal vendetta between the Mexico City mayor, Marcelo Ebrard, and the 'real' owner of El 40, an alleged ex-high ranking police officer. While the origins of the vendetta were left in the dark, the expropriation was presented as an act of punishment from the local mayor out of pure lust for personal revenge.

Following Scott, such stories can be classified as gossip. Gossip, Scott writes, 'is perhaps the most familiar and elementary form of disguised popular aggression' (Scott 1990: 142). It is a 'hidden transcript' that tells stories 'that are designed to ruin the reputation of some identifiable person or persons' in response to 'social rules that have been violated' (Scott 1990: 142). In the case of El 40, such discourses, however, were not about the violation of social rules proper. Rather, they addressed what was apparently considered to be a violation of existing *political norms* that previously defined political negotiations and interactions between the neighbourhood and the city administration. Indeed, many people considered the expropriation to be something scandalous and, through stories such as the ones described above, the perpetrators of this scandal were targeted by reputation-damaging gossip anonymously brought into circulation in the neighbourhood.

Another local response towards the expropriation consisted in different manifestations of popular art. One of these manifestations appeared in the form of a huge graffiti, close to the entrance of La Lagunilla Metro station. The graffiti politically commented on the expropriation by condemning police repression driven by overly economic interests of the local government and called residents to resist such efforts. Strategically located at a highly trafficked street, this graffiti, according to Martha, who sells soft drinks and newspapers nearby, was 'to tell them [the authorities] we're here to stay'.

Such forms of resistance spread throughout the neighbourhood, where, after the expropriation, residents of other potentially endangered housing projects, such as Casa Blanca, engaged with the local media to prevent a similar fate. They 'even hung large messages on their facades inviting the police to enter to inspect their contents, just to prove Casa Blanca was a "legitimate and clean community" and not meriting expropriation or destruction' (Davis and Ruiz de Teresa

2013: 123). This, in combination with a broader 'citizen outcry' in the aftermath of the expropriation, contributed to the fact that from nearly sixty expropriations originally planned for 2007, only five were executed, and only El 40, has been razed. In its place now is a community centre – not a gentrified urban 'enclave' – that only opened four years after the eviction took place (ibid.).

Moving beyond the particular case of the expropriation of El 40 towards more general responses of the residents of Tepito directed towards the policing-backed neoliberal upgrading of their communities, one also encounters cases of symbolic inversions through which normal social relationships and hierarchies are turned upside-down (see Scott 1990: 167–172).

A telling illustration of such practices can be found in the creation of Tepito Beach, or Tepiplaya, on calle Aztecas in April 2007. After the removal of the roofing of market stalls by the city administration, which was justified as facilitating police air surveillance of the area, the pavement of the street was completely demolished and left unfixed by the authorities. In a parody of the installation of artificial beaches throughout Mexico City in 2007 by the city administration, which drew its inspiration from similar projects in cities like Paris, local residents appropriated calle Aztecas and transformed its now sandy surface into their own version of a beach: Tepiplaya. They provided inflatable swimming pools for children, a life-guard tower and even inflatable plastic palms for the authentic beach feeling. All of this created a carnivalesque parody and subaltern political critique of both the city's own public beach project as well as the removal of the roofing and the unfulfilled promises by the local government to fix the road as soon as possible (on Tepiplaya, see also *El Universal* 2007c; *La Jornada* 2007b; Brock 2008: 216). The fact that after local news reported on the Tepiplaya, the streets were fixed and relatively quickly repaired is illustrative of the ways such practices of everyday resistance are capable of shaping and mediating the urbanization of neoliberalism in the punitive city and the constrained agency of those mostly affected by these developments.

Conclusion

Attending to the unfolding of the urbanization of neoliberalism and the related securitization of urban space in the old Merced area and the Tepito neighbourhood, this chapter offered a bottom-up perspective on the place-specificity of neoliberal urban renewal in the punitive city. The analysis stressed the mediation of larger macro-structural processes of neoliberal place-making by informal practices and multiple forms of resistance as well as contestation that are illustrative of the ongoing difficulties and the complex nature of the expansion of urban renewal, and its corresponding securitization of urban space in neighbourhoods such as the Merced or Tepito. Here local residents, as well as illegal(ized) informal economic and political actors engage in multiple forms of resistance to contest and negotiate the neoliberal 'upgrading' of their neighbourhoods and the related processes of securitization and penalization. While the chapter uncovered the agency of marginalized actors in influencing these developments, the empirical evidence presented here should not be read as a celebration of local resistance at the neighbourhood level. Not only were none of the above-mentioned practices capable of defeating top-down efforts of neoliberal place making in the punitive city. Moreover, many, if not most, of these forms of resistance, contestation and negotiation ultimately perpetuate existing local power relations and, in an ambivalent way, reinforce the penalization of poverty and marginality in contemporary Mexico City. This is because such practices of resistance generally privilege those at urban society's margins who have access to political, economic and social capital that allows them to bribe police officers, get protection from political bosses or help from politicians and bureaucrats willing to bend laws in return for political support. To put it in other terms, the rolling-out of neoliberalism in the punitive city contributes to a marginalization of the most marginal segments of the local population. Having neither the economic nor political capital to negotiate over the non-enforcement of neoliberal legislation in their favour, those people are the ones who suffer most from the punches of the 'visible fists' of the neoliberal penal state in the guise of 'repression, imprisonment, territorial sieges, and the like' (Auyero 2012: 15).

CHAPTER 4

Securitizing civic activism

In March 2006 an international conference was held in Mexico City. The two-day event under the title Foro Internacional de Convivencia Segura (International Forum for Safe Cohabitation) – organized by the Mexico City government under the direction of the SSPDF – was attended by a few hundred journalists, security practitioners, local and international academics, and many members of local NGOs. According to a press statement issued by the then-police chief, the goal of the conference was 'to exchange international public security experiences among experts'. Among the people invited to chair one of the five conference panels was María Elena Morera, by that time director of Mexico's biggest anti-crime NGO, México Unido Contra la Delincuencia, and Sigrid Arzt, an academic and founding member of another local NGO working on security issues, Democracia, Derechos Humanos y Seguridad (Democracy, Human Rights and Security), who in December of that year became the technical secretary of Mexico's National Security Council under President Felipe Calderón Hinojosa (PAN).

This event, which at first sight seems to be a typical encounter of security experts in our contemporary world, upon closer inspection can be identified as a paradigmatic symptom of a profound transformation affecting most countries in Latin America: the increasing transnationalization of security governance, most of all in the urban realm. This transnationalization is closely related to the growing importance of security-related knowledge production and expertise by

NGOs and think tanks. These actors vernacularize globally circulating security-related knowledge and practices, thereby appropriating and translating them into the local context (Merry 2005: 219). Vernarcularization, thus, is a 'process of reception and transformation, a dialectic in which transnational conceptions are made meaningful within, or rejected on the basis of, local realities – themselves already conditioned by their broader inclusion within transnational frameworks of economics, politics, and culture' (Goldstein 2012: 212).

The present chapter seeks to place the growing importance of NGOs working on security issues, as well as the related vernacularization processes, within the making of the punitive city. In doing so, the chapter sheds light on a frequently neglected aspect of the punitive turn in contemporary Latin America: the role of knowledge production and expertise that converts security experts into powerful mediators and drivers of the punitive makeover of city life in the region (on security experts as mediators, see Berling and Bueger 2015: 9–11). In fact, the securitization of urban space in contemporary Mexico City, and elsewhere in Latin America, is incomprehensible without understanding how punitive security policies, such as zero tolerance-inspired policing and legal innovations, travel South and how they get translated into local contexts by actors who, as Dezaly and Garth (2011) have argued, become veritable comprador experts engaged in the business of importing external knowledge to enhance their own power and position 'at home':

After first serving as translators, importers, and promoters of the innovations in their national spaces, these elite agents participate as local consultants for groups investigating the impact of the new governing practices. The evaluations come typically at the request of the donor organizations, and they are carried out in collaboration with those who worked with them to conceive the local projects. This collaboration is presented as the mobilization of experts from the South. The expertise comes in fact from scholarships and educational programs that bring these double agents into transnational networks organized by the learned or philanthropic organizations of the hegemonic societies. The double game they play is reminiscent of the role of intermediary and mediator filled in the past by compradors working with merchants in colonial enclaves. They introduce the colonial traders into their societies while using those from the North to enhance their own local power and profit. (Dezalay and Garth 2011: 280)

In analysing the role of security-related knowledge production, circulation and vernacularization, the chapter demonstrates how local think tanks and NGOs play a decisive role in the growing punitiveness of local politics by vernacularizing transnationally circulating security governance ideas whose incorporation into the local context provides new knowledge and legitimization narratives for the punitive makeover of the local security agenda. This process, again, is inseparable from the intersection of the democratization of local politics and the unfolding of neoliberalism, not just as an economic ideology but also as a political technology that mobilizes applied scientific expert knowledge 'pragmatically and purposefully to transform the state and society' in line with neoliberal free market ideals (Tironi and Barandiarán 2014: 305).

Moreover, the chapter also demonstrates that this vernacularization process is embedded within an externally financed boom of security-related civic activism that produced an overly competitive NGO marketplace. To be successful in this competitive market of security expertise, local NGOs must frame their funding applications in a language that is understandable for an external audience, which implies that they must demonstrate their knowledge of the state of the art of internationally circulating public security and policing knowledge, discourses and practices, while at the same time presenting themselves as politically neutral actors. This development, the chapter shows, marginalizes more politically oriented and socially embedded civic organizations with deep roots in social movements, giving the local security-related NGO community a two-tiered structure. At the top is a group of internationally connected and funded NGOs that do academic research and offer 'impartial' scientific policy advice to politicians and public institutions. At the bottom are those organizations with close connections to local communities but whose more political character makes them unattractive partners for international donors and disqualifies their 'biased' expertise for local politicians and bureaucrats. However, as the following pages will also demonstrate, this newly emerging field of transnational security expertise is dominated by informal politics, most visible in the fact that it is often not primarily the objective expertise of an NGO that translates into impact, but rather informal connections of NGO members to businessmen, politicians and bureaucrats.

Selling security in the punitive city

In 1994, three academics co-authored the first book-length academic study on public security in Mexico under PRI rule: *Seguridad Pública en México: Problemas, Perspectivas y Propuestas* (Public Security in Mexico: Problems, Perspectives and Proposals) (González Ruiz et al. 1994). The book's emphasis on *proposals* signals a major change in the local urban security field: the growing impact of security expertise and policy advice provided by actors with an academic background who were previously situated outside or at the margins of the local security field. This impact is most visible in the emergence of a community of highly transnationalized NGOs whose work focuses on security issues. The career of one of the co-authors of the previously mentioned book, Ernesto López Portillo Vargas, is telling in this regard. In the early 1990s, he joined the Instituto Nacional de Sciencias Penales (National Institute of Penal Sciences, INACIPE), a public institution created in 1976 to improve the quality of penal sciences and justice practitioners in Mexico, with one of its main tasks being the provision of academic training for (present and future) agents of the Mexican penal field. In drawing upon his security expertise gathered at INACIPE, specifically regarding international comparative security knowledge, in 2003 he founded the first Mexican NGO exclusively working on these issues, Instituto para la Seguridad y la Democracia (Institute for Security and Democracy, INSYDE), with the support of various external actors, including Open Society Institute, MacArthur Foundation, Tinker Foundation and National Endowment for Democracy.* Today, INSYDE can be considered one of Mexico's most influential and transnationally well-connected NGOs working on security issues, whose staff members (and their work) are also

---

* See also www.ifp.pgjdf.gob.mx/ifp/consejo/Cvc/ErnestoLopez.pdf.

often interviewed and cited by international academics and policy reports (see Hochmüller and Müller 2014: 712).

While there were already some civil society organizations working on issues of crime and insecurity, for instance México Unido Contra la Delincuencia (founded in 1997) or Justicia Ciudadana (Citizen Justice, founded in 1999), the foundation of INSYDE was a turning point as it became, in the words of a member of another NGO, a 'business model' that many other local academics would soon try to reproduce. As one academic stated in a personal conversation, '[w]ith INSYDE, people saw that you could sell security [to donors]'. This led to the emergence of what another interview partner from the local NGO community called a security-related 'NGO marketplace'.

This market, as the origins of INSYDE clearly illustrate, is highly transnationalized and dependent upon external funding. In this regard, another NGO member described this overall situation as the externally-funded 'constitution of an NGO market in Mexico', where it was expected 'that you can make a lot of money', while another NGO member characterized the director of his organization with the term 'entrepreneur' (*empresario*) because of his outstanding capacity to sell his projects to international donors.

The structural conditions for this market emerged in the mid-1990s. During these years, Mexico's rather weak civil society organizations received an important stimulus relating to the fact that many local organizations considered NAFTA negotiations as an opportunity to establish partnerships with US-based civic organizations and philanthropic foundations, an interest that was shared on the US side in an effort of expanding the influence over and presence within Mexican civil society within the ongoing 'democratic opening' of the country. The traditional weakness of civic society organizations in Mexico is closely related to the corporatist and clientelistic structure of the PRI regime, described in Chapter 2. In order to co-opt and control civic activism, many civic organizations were directly financed by state institutions and acted on the basis of a hidden agenda, which in many cases served particular political (and financial) goals, often related to the benefits of the dominant party. These practices have had a negative impact on the credibility and legitimacy of NGOs and prevented them from becoming deeply embedded in Mexican society. Because of this legacy, as interview partners from the local NGO community explained, Mexicans who are not directly engaged in or affected by political and social struggles often have no particular knowledge of or sympathy for such organizations nor perceive them as relevant actors for the resolution of urgent societal or political problems. In the words of one NGO member: 'NGOs have historically served to enrich those people who direct them and they aren't accountable [*han servido para enriquecer a las personas, que las dirigen y no rinden cuenta*]. Therefore people don't give [them] money, which substantially limits the amount of money you, as an organization, can expect [to receive] from the people.' As most local NGOs are aware of the historically grounded negative perception that can arise from close collaboration with public authorities, they often prefer to maintain a certain distance from public funding, This, in turn, implies that they depend on other sources of income and are therefore interested in obtaining financial resources from international donors.

From the mid-1990s onwards, the interest of US-based civic organizations in expanding their influence over, and presence within, Mexican civil society converged with the search for new funding options by Mexican actors. These interests mutually reinforced one another and contributed to a predominantly externally financed growth of civic activism in Mexico (see also Müller 2009b). In this context, external funding played a major role in nurturing civil society organizations – which in order to demonstrate their independence from the PRI regime, an interest that persisted after Vicente Fox Quesada from the PAN ousted the PRI from the presidential palace – were highly receptive to funding sources from abroad.

As a result of this, and within the context of Mexico's deteriorating security situation, and a growing concern for democratic police reform across post-authoritarian Latin America, the new millennium witnessed the growth of a Mexico City-based NGO community dedicated to issues related to security. In 2007, there were already twenty-three such NGOs working in the city, overwhelmingly funded by external actors, including state agencies, philanthropic foundations, think tanks and intergovernmental organizations. Particularly active were the World Bank, the European Commission, the MacArthur Foundation, the Tinker Foundation, the William and Flora Hewlett

Foundation, the Open Society Institute, the Ford Foundation, the Friedrich Ebert Stiftung, and the National Endowment for Democracy. What is important in this regard is that all of these external actors largely bypassed local state institutions, channelling their resources nearly exclusively to NGOs (Stanley et al. 2009).

The centrality of external funding in general, and of US foundations in particular, is widely acknowledged by the local NGO community, as well as the growing demand from Mexican civil society which has triggered an increasing competition over these resources. Recall that success in this competitive environment ultimately depends upon the ability of an NGO to submit funding applications that 'speak' the language of external donors. In practices this implies that project proposals need to be written in an overly technical language that makes constant references to globally circulating (but often unproven) international ' best practices' in the fields of security governance and policing. This in turn benefited those academics that, from a previously marginalized position within the local academic field, worked on public security or closely related issues, and were now capable of developing project proposals that by capitalizing upon their previously marginalized expertise could become involved in the newly emerging market of security expertise. This also nurtured institutional investments within the academic field in the previously marginalized area of public security, clearly visible in the burgeoning wave of publications on public security issues in the new millennium, as well as in the growing interest in public security-related academic training and study programmes.

An example of this trend is the Centro de Investigación y Docencia Económica (Centre for Research and Teaching of Economics, CIDE). CIDE is a highly internationalized public academic research and training centre with many faculty members having obtained their PhDs abroad at universities such as Oxford, Cambridge, Harvard, Stanford or the London School of Economics. CIDE also actively pursues an international publication strategy, proudly listing a huge number of prestigious international journals such as the *American Political Science Review*, *International Studies Quarterly*, or *Journal of Development Economics* as places where faculty members publish on a regular basis. In particular, CIDE's equally internationalized legal department, with only two of its eleven research professors having obtained their PhDs in Mexico, has been actively engaged in public security projects, research and teaching and even established a joint-diploma study programme in public security with INSYDE. This collaborative experience reflects a larger trend within the local academic field where investments in internationally recognized public security knowledge have become increasingly attractive and recognized by academic institutions (in particular the social sciences and legal departments) and potential students. These investments converted those actors in possession of new academic expertise – public security-related knowledge – into powerful agents within the local security field, which many of them joined by seeking employment within the new NGO sector as well as increasingly securitized academic departments and the upper levels of the public administration.

Many, if not most, of these NGOs that emerged from this academic investment in security expertise can be qualified as technocratic. Like their economic counterparts, they share a belief in and promote seemingly universally applicable legal and policing models and international best practices, while at the same time conceiving of themselves as politically neutral actors. In contrast to many civil society organizations that emerged before the 1990s, and whose members considered themselves as political activists fighting for democracy and an end of state repression in Mexico, the new security NGOs have, in the words of one NGO member, 'a more academic profile, they are more like doing research, no activism, no human rights defense work'. Central to this 'more academic profile' is the vernacularization of transnationally circulating security knowledge. As the latter is framed in the language of impartial and disinterested forms of knowledge production in the name of security best practices – and increasingly underpinned by personal contacts, joint projects and collaborations with international academics, in particular from the US* – these security technocrats, or securocrats, have been able to establish themselves as internationally

---

* An important institutionalization of such transnational academic networks has been the 'Project on Reforming the Administration of Justice in Mexico' (2002–2005) at the Center for US-Mexican Studies, University of California, San Diego (http://usmex.ucsd.edu/research/past-research-projects/justice-reforms/). Since 2005, the project, currently funded by the MacArthur Foundation, William and Flora Hewlett Foundation, Tinker Foundation, Open Society Institute, and the US Agency for International Development, is located at the Trans Border Institute, University of San Diego (http://justiceinmexico.org/).

recognized 'local' security experts. Thereby, they marginalized NGOs with a more activist and political agenda, which members of more technocratic NGOs often disqualified as a naïve 'protest attitude' and a 'wrong' emphasis on action over analysis. As in other places, this marginalization of more activist NGOs depoliticizes NGO-driven forms of civic activism through a 'professionalization of dissent' (Choudry and Kapoor 2013: 15) and nurtures 'polite reformism and self-interest in the maintenance of their organizations and funding relationships' (ibid.: 6). Moreover, this 'professionalization of dissent' further contributes to the marginalization of activist NGOs, as the more political character of the latter makes them unattractive partners for international donors and disqualifies their 'biased' expertise for local politicians and bureaucrats. In fact, the less conflictive, sensitive and political the issue is in the eyes of politicians and bureaucrats, the higher the likelihood that the latter will collaborate and engage with an NGO. This is indicative of the political economy operative in the Mexico City NGO marketplace, and the frequently observed complicity with state institutions, which produces 'forms of hegemonic NGO politics', 'wherein the terms of social change amount to limited gains as opportunities might permit *within* existing structures' (Choudry and Kapoor 2013: 5, original emphasis). As a staff member of a more activist NGO commented in this respect: 'Analysis does not hurt the government, it only produces words that can easily be ignored. More action, most of all legal action is what we need.'

The reward for the professionalization of dissent, as argued above, is open doors to state institutions, which, in turn, represent symbolic capital for NGOs, as this can be sold to donors as a guarantee that funding will have a transformative impact. However, a closer look at the realities in Mexico City shows that this impact hardly materializes because 'open doors' are often a means of cooptation that allows public authorities to manage security experts and appropriate their knowledge while demonstrating a general willingness to collaborate with civil society.

The activities of the SSPDF in response to the growing presence of security NGOs are a telling illustration of this. Since the early 2000s, the SSPDF became more open to collaboration with NGOs and academics, including an academic exchange programme between the country's most renowned public university, the Universidad Nacional Autonóma de México (National Autonomous University of Mexico), and the local police academy in April 2012, as well as the organization of a variety of international exchanges and conferences. In addition to this, the SSPDF increasingly embraced international policing best practices, in particular community policing, which is promoted by many local NGOs and academics as the best way to democratize local policing and for making it more accountable. In addition to the *policía de barrio* project, mentioned in Chapter 2, which was inaugurated in 2004, this took the form of the creation of the UPCs, mentioned in Chapter 1, operating in Mexico City since 2002. In interviews, bureaucrats and members from the NGO community frequently referred to these policing imports as purely symbolic actions, aimed at publicly demonstrating that through the import of internationally recognized best practices the local PRD administration is taking seriously the security concerns of the local electorate, with the UPCs being, in the words of a former high-ranking security bureaucrat, '[t] he best example of such a show'. While this seems undeniable, these imports cannot be reduced to electoral politics. Rather, they also reflect the vernacularization of new, inherently transnational, security knowledge that has been introduced into the local context by NGOs and their vision of legitimate policing practice, thereby forcing the SSPDF to increasingly adapt to this new policing worldview. The UPCs are a case in point that illustrates how orthodox actors inside the police apparatus were forced to re-frame their policing worldview because of the growing legitimacy of the new policing visions introduced into the field by security NGOs and academics. The UPCs were invented by a military general in his seventies who had already served during the height of PRI repression in the 1960s and 1970s. Despite the fact that, in the words of one NGO member, the general 'has a vision [of policing] that is completely different [from ours, that of the NGO], a vision based on his experience under the dictatorship', he was nonetheless forced to contribute to the local police reform agenda by appropriating the worldview of the new policing 'heretics' and their special emphasis on community-oriented policing programmes.

The abovementioned efforts by the SSPDF to confront the challenge posed by a growing community of security NGOs (and academics) can be interpreted as efforts of symbolic capital accumulation through 'co-optation, understood as the circular relations of reciprocal recognition among peers' (Bourdieu 1993: 116). This strategy is marked by a 'double game'. On the one hand, the SSPDF officially recognizes the expertise of security NGOs and academics by publicly performing an interest in fostering collaboration 'among peers', which promises access to their symbolic credentials in the guise of international security expertise. On the other hand, however, the SSPDF tries to appropriate the NGO's symbolic capital without giving them too much access to and insights (and impact) on the institution itself. For instance, the above quoted NGO member who worked on the UPCs stated that the interview responses they got from UPC members were influenced by their superiors: 'We have noted an effort from the Secretariat [of Public Security], from the general [who created the UPCs], to influence the answers the interviewees would give us.' Other NGO members and academics referred to similar experiences, indicating that in collaborating with the new 'heretics', the SSPDF's effort of symbolic capital accumulation through co-optation in practice takes the form of a strategically controlled embrace.

Other efforts of building up symbolic capital focused on substantial investments in the technological modernization of the local police forces through the purchase of the latest in computer software and surveillance technology. Moreover, as part of an integral administrative reform within the local bureaucratic field, many middle and upper ranks within the administration of the penal apparatus, in particular those related to information technology and public management, were increasingly staffed with graduates from the abovementioned security-oriented academic training programmes, that is with people capable of managing, implementing and performing according to the standards of international best practices, providing the administrative arms of the bureaucratic field with what one interview partner called a more 'academic touch', thereby bringing in, while at the same time recognizing, prestigious symbolic capital in the guise of academic security expertise. Finally, the SSPDF's strategy is also visible in its police training efforts. For instance, the local police academy now regularly offers training courses in collaboration with internationally recognized police institutions, such as the Federal Bureau of Investigation, and its curriculum includes courses on community policing as well as on the implications of the Giuliani report regarding the import of zero tolerance policing (SSPDF 2006: 351–356).

The incorporation of the recommendations of the Giuliani report (see Chapter 1) into the police training curriculum is illustrative of the contribution the vernacularization of transnational security expertise by local NGOs, think tanks and philanthropic foundations has made to the punitive turn in Mexico City politics and the underlying securitization of urban space. In fact, NGOs like México Unido Contra la Delincuencia, as well as the Instituto Cultural Ludwig von Mises (Cultural Institute Ludwig von Mises) – founded in 1983 by economist Bettina Bien Greaves, an active promoter of neoliberal free-market ideals, in order to offer intellectual support for the neoliberal turn in Mexican politics (Plehwe 2001) – actively participated in the vernacularization of punitive security knowledge by contributing to the diffusion of repressive urban policing models such as zero tolerance policing. For instance, both organizations invited George Kelling to conferences in Mexico City in 2000. Kelling, a professor at Rutgers University and Senior Fellow at the conservative think-tank Manhattan Institute, is one of the founding fathers of the broken windows theory, which argues 'that the unchallenged presence of minor visible signs of social and physical disorder could lead to more serious crime problems' (Vitale 2008: 46), and that, as is well known, serves as the ideological underpinning of zero tolerance policing (see chapter 1). The Instituo Cultural Ludwig von Mises even published a Spanish translation of *Fixing Broken Windows*, a book co-authored by Kelling and Catherine M. Coles in 2001 for the Mexican book market (see also Wacquant 2009a: 169–170). Thus, as elsewhere, in Mexico City 'the role of think tanks has been pivotal to the diffusion of aggressive penality "made in the USA"' and the merging of a neoliberal political economy symbolized by the 'Chicago Boys' and an economy of security expertise promoted by the 'New York Boys', most notably Rudolph Giuliani and his police chief William Bratton (Wacquant 2009b: 167–168).

As argued in chapter 1, in Mexico City, this merging was not accidental. Rather, it was the main objective of the Giuliani initiative, because the private sector and the PRD administration, rightly, assumed that a consultancy contract with Giuliani Partners would provide for a locally attuned version of zero tolerance policing that would help to speed-up the neoliberal 'rescue' of downtown Mexico City. As this rescue project is the single most important manifestation of the punitive makeover of urban governance in neoliberal Mexico City, it illustrates the impact the vernacularization of transnationally circulating security knowledge had in the making of the punitive city.

A closely related process can be observed with regard to the at first sight more empowering discourse of 'citizen security' (*seguridad ciudadana*), a concept that has become the new buzzword in the realm of urban security governance in Mexico City, and elsewhere in Latin America (Goldstein 2012; Hochmüller and Müller 2016). While most local security NGOs promote the concept and present citizen security as the most democratic way of public security provision by de facto arguing for a *right* to security, it should be noted that, as Goldstein has shown for the case of Bolivia, citizen security's 'emphasis on security serves to introduce a new kind of right into the global debate over the meaning of human rights – the right to security – which shifts local understandings of human rights in ways that are potentially violent and at odds with normative transnational human rights ideals' (Goldstein 2012: 204). The fact that the concept of citizen security has been incorporated into the LCC, which, as argued in Chapter 1, is *the* main legal instrument for the security-related safeguarding of neoliberal urban renewal in the city, clearly demonstrates that the framing of security as a right for local residents to which they are legally entitled qua their status as citizens, furthermore contributes to the punitive remaking of local politics and the conversion of rule of law discourses into rule through law practices. Indeed, the at first sight empowering idea of declaring security as a right for citizens, at a closer look divides up the space of society into an antagonistic camp with the idea of 'rights-deserving' citizens on one side, and 'punishment-deserving' non-citizen criminal others on the other. In vernacularizing transnational security discourses and practices, from zero tolerance to citizen security, transnationalized security NGOs in Mexico City have thus become de facto force multipliers of the punitive governing of urban marginality by introducing and legitimizing new forms of punitive urban security governance practices in the local context.

Playing the NGO game

As the reference to Pierre Bourdieu's concept of 'symbolic capital' and the idea of symbolic capital accumulation in the previous section indicates, when seen through the conceptual apparatus of Bourdieu's work, the security NGO community in Mexico City can be analysed as a 'field'. The notion of the field has been introduced by Bourdieu in order to develop a relational understanding of the social world. Fields are sites of struggles in and through which involved actors and institutions try to modify/perpetuate a given constellation of forces and the relations of domination/subordination operating in the field by altering/maintaining the distribution of field-specific (material, symbolic and incorporated) power resources that Bourdieu calls *capital*. The following quote summarizes these basic properties of a field:

> In analytical terms, a field may be defined as a network, or a configuration, of objective relations between positions. These positions are objectively defined, in their existence and in the determinations they impose upon their occupants, agents or institutions, by their present and potential situation (*situ*) in the structure of the distribution of species of power (or capital) whose possession commands access to the specific profits that are at stake in the field, as well as by their objective relation to other positions (domination, subordination, homology, etc.). (Bourdieu and Wacquant 1992: 97)

Despite the emphasis in this quote on 'objectively defined' relations, Bourdieu's understanding of the field implies that the latter does not exist beyond agency nor the properties and investments agents make in order to play in the field (Bigo 2011: 239). However, in order to participate in the particular struggles, or the 'game', taking place in a given field, actors must have a shared 'feel of the game' or a 'practical sense' of what actually is at stake in the field (Bourdieu 1990: 68).

The practical sense required for playing the security NGO-game in contemporary Mexico City implies a feel for the workings of power in the informal political universe that shapes urban security governance in the punitive city. While it is the stated goal of all interviewed NGOs to influence and improve the practices of public institutions, such efforts, in fact, are mediated and overdetermined by the social and political capital that a particular NGO represents for politicians and bureaucrats. As one interviewee put it:

Well, what I'm trying to say is that the differences between the NGOs and their different profiles affect their access to the public authorities. For example, for an organization of indigenous people from Chiapas, it will be very difficult to gain access to the President, because they are living in different worlds, in very distant worlds. On the other hand, an organization of wealthy people, dedicating their work to street children, will, with a very high probability, get this access, no? To a certain degree, access to the institutions depends on the persons who constitute the NGOs, but also on the profile of the organizations. [...] From what we have seen, the only pattern [regarding NGOs' access to public authorities] is on the one hand related to the composition of the organizations, socio-economic, intellectual and ideological. On the other hand, it [NGOs' access to public authorities] depends on the goals [of the NGOs]. I think that with these two dimensions [in mind] you can make a very sincere map that shows how much access they have [to public authorities] and how much access to authorities they need for their work.

This passage clearly demonstrates how the social, symbolic and political capital associated with a particular NGO, its member composition and agenda, affects the potential access to state officials and politicians. Social capital, defined as 'the sum of the resources, actual or virtual, that accrue to an individual or a group by virtue of possessing a durable network of more or less institutionalized relationships of mutual acquaintance and recognition' (Bourdieu and Wacquant 1992: 119), is a particularly important resource in this regard, as the following passage with another NGO member illustrates:

Well, Mexican foundations, the philanthrophic sector in Mexico, partly because of the problem of the NGOs [their historical proximity to the government] and in part because of deep cultural problems [*problemas culturales muy de fondo*], they give money to people whom they know. Therefore it [funding] continues to be dependent upon godfathers [*compadres*] and friends. So if you have a friend who knows the owner of a company [and] who knows the foundation, they will give you money. And if you don't know him, even if your project is very good, they won't give you money.

As these two interview passages demonstrate, informal practices based on social and political (as well as symbolic) capital are key factors for successfully joining the security NGO game in Mexico City. It is through the possession of social capital and political capital that funding from Mexican foundations can be attracted and access to public authorities be established. However, informally established access to public authorities does not necessarily translate into the impact NGOs and donors would wish for.

In fact, most NGO members I interviewed expressed a high degree of frustration regarding the unwillingness of local politicians and members of the institutions of the administration of justice to comply with the promises made to NGOs. This lack of compliance was explained with the same factors that enable these NGOs to obtain funding and establish contacts to local authorities: clientelistic relations, friendships and godparents. These factors offer protection to friends from NGO criticism and from outsiders' interference with one's own agenda. Faced with this situation, some local NGOs appealed to international institutions, such as the Inter-American Court of Human-Rights, in order to put pressure on state actors and institutions. However, even the launching of this strategy, which has been termed the 'boomerang effect' because 'domestic NGOs bypass their state and directly search out international allies to try to bring pressure on their states from outside' (Keck and Sikkink 1998: 12), is no guarantee that local authorities will react positively. The following lengthy citation from an interview with a member of a local NGO focused on legal actions against human rights abuses offers an appropriate description of the magnitude of obstacles involved in such processes of making (international and national) human rights standards work in Mexico by opting for this boomerang strategy:

> What is true is that the state listens to you, but it does not comply. In Mexico there is no legal system that would apply international [human rights] recommendations or decisions to the national level. This means that it [the international human rights system] only serves as a medium for political pressure. Unfortunately, in our legal environment there exists no possibility of applying international criteria to concrete legal cases. Despite the fact that our constitution gives international treaties the status of supreme laws, there are no institutional juridical mechanisms that permit the direct application of a decision. [...] The possibility to sanction high-ranking police personnel when they or the officers under their command commit human rights violations is confronted with serious structural problems. First, the Mexican justice system. Here, first of all the public prosecutor [*ministerio público*] has to prove the subjective responsibility and the type of offence. Although a woman [...] could state that: I was violated so and so, but I cannot identify the aggressor because they covered my eyes and I was in a dark bus. Nevertheless, I know that these 20 men were in the bus. Who of them violated me, well I don't know, but it is certain that other testimonies support my declaration, but due to the fact that I could not identify my aggressor, this declaration will not be processed. What I am trying to explain is that whenever there is no individual responsibility with first-name and last-name, judicial sanctions will not be applied. Now, in the estimated case that the victim recognized her aggressor, let's say the police agent Juan Pérez, as long as he does not testify that he received an order from his superiors to violate that woman in this particular moment, there is no legal responsibility from his superiors, and when there is no legal responsibility, there is also no political responsibility. Because in order to sanction a governor or a police chief of whom we know that he gave the orders for this operation, you need a political judgement [*juicio*

político] from the legislative power of the respective state or from the federal level. But, for sure, this guy has his godfathers [*compadres*] among the deputies, and they won't prosecute him. So, there is no way, definitely no way to sanction neither high-ranking police officers, nor the responsible politicians.

To overcome such problems, local NGOs often develop more informal strategies for gaining access to public authorities. Such strategies are most often centred on the establishment of good personal contacts, which some interviewees referred to as friendships, with key persons in state bureaucracies. In addition to this, another option for local NGOs to improve their access to local institutions, and the responsiveness of the latter, is the strategy of luring institutional personel by presenting collaboration with NGOs as useful for their future (political) career. As one informant described it: 'You have to understand that politicians have their own agenda. You have to look where points of convergence are and these have to be taken up.'

Through such practices, NGOs not only join the 'game' at play in the local field of security knowledge production; they also contribute to the wider reproduction of informal politics and practices that shape urban security governance in the punitive city, not at least because informal practices and social capital also often affect the internal practices of local NGOs. In this regard, interview partners mentioned that personnel recruitment and employment options of local NGOs are also frequently based on personal relationships and not on the particular qualification of the employed persons.

In light of the above, the overall contribution of such transnationalized security NGOs to security governance in Mexico City has not so much been the improvement of the local security situation. Rather, they have introduced new forms of punitive security knowledge and practices into a local security field, while reproducing the informal practices that have historically shaped urban security governance in the city (see Chapter 2). As recent studies have demonstrated, after fifteen years of urban democracy and the vernacularization of transnational security expertise, the logics of routine policing and law enforcement – including the imported international 'best practices' – continue to be dominated by informality, patronage, arbitrariness, human rights violations and the involvement in criminal activities (Azaola and Ruiz Torres 2011; Fondevila 2011; Uildriks 2010; Müller 2012a). That the local security situation has hardly improved under these conditions is not very surprising and is clearly visible in the fact that local residents continue to imagine their city as one of the most unsafe urban places in the country.

The seeming paradox behind this situation is that Mexico City's transnational urban security field is what Dezalay and Garth, in their analysis of externally imported rule of law reforms in Latin America, have called a 'two-tiered system'. This system is comprised of a cosmopolitan elite propagating and importing 'grand principles' at the top and 'ordinary' agents, actors and bureaucrats at the bottom, whose routine practices continue to be defined by 'clientelism and patronage' (Dezalay and Garth 2002: 249). These two tiers are so socially and institutionally separated that the impact of the transnational elite on improving local practices is extremely limited. In a telling passage they write:

> The cosmopolitan importers work to construct a new, internationally acceptable and legitimate state, but they must confront deeply ingrained practices at all social levels and the people who sustain those practices in ways that ultimately benefit the cosmopolitan elite. [...] The devalorization or disqualification of local justice and local states in Latin America (and elsewhere) because of their embeddedness in patronage and clientelism also provides legitimacy and prestige for those at the top of the two-tiered system. They gain recognition, in part, for their sophistication of their criticisms. Their distance and their cosmopolitan connections and credibility, in other words, allow them to appear as a nobility speaking on behalf of the new sophisticated remedies for the state and the economy. (Dezalay and Garth 2002: 248–249)

While in Mexico City, the gap between the two tiers of this system is not as big as Dezalay and Garth suggest, and 'clientelism and patronage' are not the exclusive privilege of those actors situated at the bottom of the security field, the overall scenario described in this quote very well captures the realities of the limited impact and logics operative in the field of security NGO expertise in Mexico City, where none of the vernacularized international best practices 'trickled down' in a way that would have contributed to an improvement of the local security situation.

However, it seems unlikely that the emerging market for transnational security experts in Mexico City, as well as the normative visions praising and driving this process, will soon wither away despite the apparent failure in improving the local security situation. In fact, it is precisely the failure of the previous vernacularization efforts to contribute to such an outcome that, as Dezalay and Garth point out, provides endless opportunities for bureaucratic, academic, political and civil society elites to invest in the newest internationally circulating forms of knowledge in order to improve their power within the local security field. In this regard, these 'politics of failure' (Moe 2016) trigger a potentially endless circle of improvement through internationalization/vernacularization: 'The perception of failure, however, also provides an opportunity for new generations. Each new cosmopolitan generation coming to power can invest in the need to complete the previous generation's unfinished business' (Dezalay and Garth 2002: 50). Moreover, as the vernacularization of international security governance 'best practices' provides local politicians interested in 'making crime pay', in political and economic terms, with important discursive and practical tools for the punitive governing of marginality, the demand for such forms of expertise is unlikely to decrease in the foreseeable future.

Conclusion

In analysing the emergence of a community of security NGOs, this chapter has demonstrated how the vernacularization of transnational forms of security knowledge, far from improving the local security situation, actually reinforced the punitive tendencies of urban governance in contemporary Mexico City. In this regard, the chapter has shown the implicit and explicit complicity of securitizing civic activism in the making of the punitive city. The more explicit contribution security NGOs make to the punitive turn in local politics consists of the facilitation of the import of punitive policing models, such as zero tolerance policing. The implicit side of this process relates to the tactical uses of informal and highly personalistic practices that NGOs engage with in order to attract funding, recruit staff members and establish contacts to politicians and bureaucrats.

In addition to this, the weakness of the local civil society and its internal dynamics, as well as the dependence of NGOs on external funding, have put additional constraints on the impact of organized security-related civic activism for an improvement of the local security situation.

However, as security expertise has become an attractive commodity that can be sold to local politicians, international donors and funding agencies eager to improve and democratize security governance in Mexico City, the limited impact of security-related civic activism offers security NGO entrepreneurs endless opportunities for accumulating symbolic, social, political and economic capital by vernacularizing transnationally circulating security best practices, and literally selling their own expertise on an increasingly competitive NGO marketplace. However, as the next chapter will demonstrate, the marketization of security in the punitive city not only refers to security-related forms of knowledge production and civic activism. The local insecurity situation has triggered a much broader boom of formal and informal forms of commodified security as well as protection practices that in many ways further contribute to the marginalizing and exclusionary tendencies operating in the punitive city.

CHAPTER 5

Self-policing, commodified protection and community justice

One of the most neglected aspects of current studies on urban (in)security in Latin America's 'violent democracies' is the growing proliferation of neoliberal forms of self-help, ranging from commodified protection to more informal bottom-up practices, such as lynchings and vigilante justice (but see Goldstein 2012, 2004). This chapter provides an overview of these developments in Mexico City and points towards their consequences for, as well as contributions to, the making of the punitive city. While the growing presence of private security guards on the streets of Mexico City as well as the growth of gated communities – and other security enclaves, such as shopping malls – represents the most iconic manifestation of the privatization of security in neoliberal Mexico City, the chapter moves beyond purely commodified forms of private protection to address the quotidian micropolitics of security in the city. These micropolitics include forms of individual self-policing, the privatization of public security, as well as a variety of less benign activities such as vigilantism and lynchings, very often related to forms of indigenous justice. The chapter demonstrates that the proliferation of these activities throughout Mexico City produces a fragmentation of urban spaces and increasingly leads urban denizens to reduce and avoid contacts with an unknown 'urban other' out of the fear of becoming victimized. This not only has negative consequences for the everyday sociability of urban society: the underlying and resulting climate of fear, in turn, is also a productive breeding ground for penal populism and 'tough on crime' politics, discussed in Chapter 1, which further reinforce the growing punitiveness of Mexico City's neoliberal urban democracy that, as this chapter indicates, increasingly expands into everyday social relations in the city.

Self-policing in Mexico City

When I first arrived in Mexico City, in the spring of 2006, my flatmate asked me not to answer the phone with my name and not to give her name or address to an unknown caller – no matter which institution or company this person might claim to represent. Similar requests were made from different people throughout my entire fieldwork. I was advised not to carry too much cash with me and to leave my credit card at home whenever possible. I was warned not to walk alone in the streets after dark nor to take a taxi on the streets at night, and when I had to do so it was suggested that I should prove the authenticity of its license plate and the driver's 'authenticity card'. I was advised not to travel with my laptop on public transport, and some people even recommended avoiding public transport altogether. This personal experience is indicative of one central aspect of Mexico City's contemporary security context, which can be described as a form of self-policing: the regulation and limitation of one's own conduct and activities in public and private spaces due to security concerns. In other words, self-policing 'tends to give rise to a strict overseer type of relation to the self which precludes spontaneity' (O'Grady 2005: 122), in this case, out of the fear of becoming a victim of crime.

In order to address the issue of self-policing beyond anecdotal evidence, it makes sense to turn to a representative survey on urban insecurity (ICESI 2008). The study not only provides evidence regarding the widespread fear of crime in urban Mexico, it also concentrates on the responses by urban residents to confront this situation. In this regard, the study shows that due to the fear of becoming a victim of crime, urban residents have stopped wearing jewellery (56 per cent) and have left their credit and debit cards at home (38 per cent). Some residents have stopped using taxis (37 per cent), while others have stopped going out at night (49.1 per cent), even no longer visiting friends and relatives (30.5 per cent). While the survey presents the related information in a very general way and does not disaggregate the data for individual cities, such practices can also been observed for Mexico City (see also Becerra Sánchez 2007: 127–29). The following passage drawn from an interview with a forty-one-year-old housewife, is paradigmatic in this respect: 'Whenever you have to go out at night, we all walk the streets in fear. You are imprisoned. You have to walk in fear. I walk in fear, but once I used to walk all night long on the streets here in this area of our neighbourhood.'

As a consequence of an ever present concern of becoming a victim of crime, this form of self-policing affects how people perceive the urban environment, the ways they interact with each other in their daily routines, and how they construct social relationships. Local residents not only decide to stop visiting friends or family members, they are also more cautious and anxious in their everyday encounters with others. In a social context where, in principle, everyone unknown is expected to be a potential security threat, many people not only 'bury themselves in their homes', as one interviewee put it, but also tend to reduce their contact with other people, and carefully evaluate the risks involved in such interactions. The following interview passage with a local businessman demonstrates such perceptions:

> Sometimes, in your conversation with other people, you tell many things: 'Look at my house, I will do this and that, my daughter goes to this place'. You simply start talking, but this is where we must be very cautious. [...] You'll never know how this turns out. It can be you are talking with a person who seems to be a really nice guy, but in reality he's only checking out your possessions.

Such perceptions, and the related modifications of people's habits, not only diminish interactions with others, they also have negative effects on the sociability that could arise from everyday encounters in the public spaces of Mexico City. Self-policing – be it in its most radical way of trying not to leave one's home whenever possible, or in its more quotidian manifestations such as avoiding public spaces by moving around in one's car or by permanently calculating whether it might be safe or unsafe to use this or that street – contributes to a growing social distance and mistrust among the city's inhabitants. Self-policing thus discourages 'the interaction with "others" from different social backgrounds' leading to a 'favouring of security above contact' (Pansters and Castillo Berthier 2007: 36–37). Through this securitization of urban space 'from below', the urban other becomes the unknown, the mistrusted, the suspicious and potentially criminal, because the other is not experienced in the daily routines and inter-actions of many local residents, which increasingly take place behind closed doors leading to an increasing abandonment of public streets and sidewalks.

According to Jane Jacobs (1961: chapter 2), public streets and sidewalks are essential elements for the construction of a secure and inclusive urban environment. On the one hand, they permit the free interaction of strangers. On the other hand, they produce forms of 'mutual policing' (ibid.: 36), an observation that she coined in the call: 'everyone must use the streets' ibid. Following Jacobs' argument, we can conclude that the growing self-segregation of people living in Mexico City, as expressed in forms of self-policing, clearly under-mines such security potentials. Moreover, as this securitization 'from below' often portrays city streets and/or particular neighbourhoods as unsafe and insecure places better to be avoided by local residents, these urban spaces also lose their potential to produce natural forms of mutual policing and everyday encounters with strangers – devoid of fear and anxiety, thereby strengthening the climate of fear that substantially contributes to the rise of punitive politics in the city (see Chapter 1).

While such individual and, indeed, individualizing forms of self-policing are undeniable, it makes sense to broaden the abovemen-tioned definition of self-policing by including also more collective ways in which groups of people come together in order to provide security and protection for themselves. The most common forms of such collective self-policing efforts in Mexico City can be found at the neighbourhood level. Some examples include the exchange of tele-phone and cell phone numbers among the residents of the same street in order to inform each other in the case of an emergency or the presence of suspicious persons, or in areas with little or no street lighting people try to coordinate their journey home from work so that they do not have to walk the poorly lit streets alone after dark. Similar practices were also described by local shopkeepers, who often keep an eye on each other's businesses and, in the case of a suspicious event, robbery or assault, inform the surrounding businesses and call the police. Such practices were also mentioned by many local residents, in particular those living in more densely populated marginalized neighbourhoods, the so-called *colonias populares*. In the words of a local resident living in Iztapalapa, one of the most marginalized boroughs of Mexico City: '[O]nce you have been accepted [in your neighbourhood], once you are known and have relations with the neighbours, this provides you with a certain support and security, a level of mutual solidarity amongst ourselves.' As this quotation illustrates, one basic precondition for the emergence of such collective protection practices is a high level of social cohesion at the neighbourhood level. Although such efforts can make a positive contribution to the local (in)security situation, collective forms of self-policing in communities with a high level of social cohesion are not just idyllic forms of security provision 'from below'. Rather, they function on the basis of symbolic and disciplinary power, often creating perceptions of permanent informal surveillance. Such forms of self-policing, therefore, also include the informal imposition of dominant local and moral norms and lifestyles. This cannot only become a permanent source of conflict – frequently in generational and/or gendered terms – but also an important factor behind the decision of local residents *not* to seek assistance from the public authorities. In the words of a resident from a poor Mexico City neighbourhood:

If I go and accuse somebody from here, well the fight isn't going to just end there. If it were somebody from outside, from another *colonia* who has come to look for trouble, you go and you file a complaint. You go and accuse him, that's how the legal procedure works. But in the case of someone from the same *colonia*, you are going to have a constant fight, an interminable fight, because the dispute will no longer just be with him but with his mother, with his father, with his family. And it is something you are going to have to deal with day in and day out. As a result you prefer to just say, 'It was the fight, this jerk was just drunk, he was on drugs'. But you decide to just leave it at that, to that night's fight, because otherwise it becomes something bigger that goes beyond what happened.

In other words, the search for protection 'beyond the state' through forms of collective self-policing is not only associated with problems related to inefficient, corrupt and/or violent police forces. Accordingly, it also mirrors the social constraints placed on local residents in neighbourhoods with very dense levels of internal social cohesion and social control to seek the assistance of public institutions in order to avoid a perpetuation, if not escalation, of the related problems.

However, there are also forms of active, although frequently informal, participation of public authorities within collective self-policing efforts. A telling example can be found in the widespread phenomenon of closed streets (*calles cerradas*). These streets have been blocked, for example through chains, bars and other obstacles, by local residents in order to impede and/or regulate the entry of unknown persons and vehicles.

Such closures, which are usually done out of security concerns, are illegal; although they are largely tolerated due to political calculations by and informal negotiations with public authorities, frequently the local borough mayors and/or their representatives (Müller 2012c: 118-120).

In interviews, local residents also have reported that in cases of serious crimes, such as rape, homicide or fights involving excessive violence, they would seek the assistance of the police. This decision equally demonstrates the incapacity of micro-level security and protection arrangements to deal with such crimes, as well as efforts by the local community to preserve the integrity of neighbourhood relations by intentionally externalizing the conflict resolution to a public authority, perceived as standing above particular interests – notwithstanding negative personal experiences with the police (see also Müller 2012d; 342-343; Tello 2012: 21).

An interesting and paradigmatic example can be found in the case of the territory governed by the left-wing political group Frente

Popular Francisco Villa Independiente UNOPI (Independent Popular Front Francisco Villa UNOPI, FPFVI). Although this is an autonomous, self-governed space – whose governance structure includes the question of security provision – inside Iztapalapa, which a member of the local administration of justice called a 'lost territory for the state', there are cases in which the administration of justice by the FPFVI encounters problems that cannot be resolved without the participation of the police – as a public security provider. The territory under the authority of the FPFVI was taken over by the organization in 1994. It now comprises around eight hectares of land on which some 4,000 people live. The *colonia* provides housing and free infrastructure for its residents, including water and electricity, their own school and even a community radio. Additionally, the FPFVI also has its own security structure. For example, there is a permanent presence of guards at the two main entrances of the *colonia* who check and question everyone wanting to enter. Each member of the FPFVI is obliged to do a guard service once a month. In this respect, the people are organised in twenty-eight brigades, and each brigade is responsible for one day of guard service. The daily shifts, always covered by at least five members of the respective brigade, are divided into three. The first shift is from 6 a.m. to 2 p.m., the second shift from 2 p.m. to 10 p.m., and the night shift is from 10 p.m. to 6 a.m. Besides the guard system, there is also an alarm whistle that can be used by all members in order to inform and mobilize them in the case of an emergency – including any questions of insecurity. The following, longer account from an interview with a member of the FPFVI not only gives us an impression of how justice is administered in the *colonia*, it additionally confronts us with a perception of where this kind of administration of justice 'beyond the state' encounters its limits. Asked if there were cases when the FPFVI would decide to bring in public authorities, the interviewed FPFVI member gave the following response:

> Yes there are. When, for example, someone from the outside comes in and robs, he tries to rob a water tank or break into a house, so they get in, but the people stop them. So what do we do? One day they caught somebody and they took away his clothes and hung a sign on him that said: 'I am a thief',

and they took him on a walk all over the neighbourhood so that people could see that he was a thief. In some cases some of the guys will give him a few slaps in the face and throw him out, because the problem isn't very big. At one point there was another type of internal problem. For example, one of the *compañeros* raped a 4 year-old girl, here inside. So the mother denounced him. The people were outraged by this. They beat him up, but we decided to hand him over to the police because in the end we can have our own rules. We can have a different vision [of justice], but there are some cases where we can't go beyond what exists, so the law that exists is the only one. The other option was to leave him at the hands of the people, and this would have generated a quite different situation. So what happened was that the police were called. Those in the patrol cars know that they can't come in here. They come and they wait at the door and they knock… like this: 'I am here to hand over a notice', or to to ask what is happening. So they inform us and we receive them here. For instance, this rapist was handed over to the police. We've called them, we said that we have this guy, that we will wait for them at the door, we handed the person over and they took him away. So there are questions like this. I don't know, for example some youth are fighting in the doorway, they pull out a gun and shoot at each other. In that case we don't expose ourselves either. What we do is keep the door closed and we call [the police] and say: 'This and this is happening. Come over here and solve it.' So yes, there are times when we resort to the authorities and ask them [for help], for example as in the case of the rapist. Often this type of people [*este tipo de gente*] they are put in jail and four days later they're again free, because their family members pay a bribe and he gets free without any problem. So what we do as an organization, is to go the borough administration and demand that they comply with the law. Although in that case, it didn't go well [*nos salió mal*] because they took the guy, this rapist, and on the way to the delegación, in the police car, he arrived dead.

This interview passage not only demonstrates how a particular private regime of punishment works in contemporary Mexico City, it also demonstrates in a paradigmatic way that existing informal security arrangements at the neighbourhood level, at one point or another, are dependent on state resources in order to solve security problems or conflicts whose resolution is perceived as being beyond the capacities of these arrangements. In such cases, and notwithstanding the negative perceptions about the local police, the active engagement of the police as a *public* institution was presented as a frequently successful and important security strategy. In these cases, police intervention not only resolves the immediate security problem, it also permits that the conflictive situation does not explode, thereby protecting the integrity of social relations at the neighbourhood level by externalizing and displacing the respective problem and its disruptive potential. Moreover, this passage also demonstrates the punitive consequences of such forms of collective self-policing that, in this case even led to the death of the presumed rapist.

By adding another informal dimension to the repertoire of, in that case ultimately lethal, punitive politics in contemporary Mexico City, communities engaging in practices of local justice are, in fact, often also active agents of the punitive turn in local politics. Far from representing empowering bottom-up responses to insecurity and problems of the local police forces, the community justice they administer is not impartial or neutral. It is power-laden, and reflects dominant moral values and visions of order. In similar ways as the formal administration of justice, such forms of bottom-up approaches are likely to marginalize the most marginalized groups inside a given community, often women and male youth. Moreover, their legally plural nature in fact allows for the appropriation and integration of the repressive forms of state-sanctioned rule of law, thereby merging formal and informal means of repression and punishment in a way that those at the receiving end of community justice suffer from the worst of both legal worlds. The implicit complicity of public authorities in this outcome will be further illustrated in the next section, where the intentional privatization of, formal and informal, policing and protection in the punitive city will be assessed.

The informal privatization of policing

When addressing the privatization of protection in contemporary Mexico City, it is important to analytically differentiate between more informal processes related to the privatization of public policing, on the one hand, and the growing commodification of security and protection, as exemplified in the recent boom of private security companies and gated communities, on the other. Although the distinction between formal and informal private policing is not common within the related literature, this distinction is pertinent for the analysis of protection in the case of Mexico City, a context where, as the previous chapters have already demonstrated, 'political actors often play by informal rules of the game' (Levitsky and Murillo 2005: 273). This observation not only captures the practices of, for example, bureaucrats, politicians and political parties, it also describes a decisive feature of Mexico City policing, thereby contributing to the informal privatization of public policing.

The latter is inseparable from a deeply embedded informal police culture, patronage structures and inner-institutional payoff systems that emerged after the Mexican Revolution and that still continue to overdetermine policing in contemporary Mexico City (see Müller 2013a, 2012c; Azaola and Ruiz Torres 2011; Uildriks 2010; Davis 2010). As one related study has summed up: 'Among those who are trying to address high levels of crime in Mexico City, there is a shared sentiment of hopelessness sustained by the perception that the law enforcement system is completely corrupt' (Anozie et al. 2004: 2). As a result, local residents are well aware of the possibility of privatizing policing through monetary and/or non-monetary incentives. In actively exploiting these opportunities in their daily lives, it is not uncommon that citizens 'resolve violations of the law at the street level through coercive bribery rather than through juridical procedures guaranteed by the formal justice system' (Davis 2010: 49).

In fact, local residents often reported that police officers were 'bought' in order to solve personal problems, such as family conflicts or problems with neighbours, by bribing local police officers in order to resolve their problems, to intimidate their opponents or to punish someone by using their coercive and/or legal faculties. Such forms of converting police officers into personal problem solvers and enforcers of private interests were described as particularly threatening when the respective police officers intervened as 'punishers' on the basis of friendship or due to family ties, as the following interview account demonstrates:

> A neighbour, the wife of a member of the Judicial Police, had a verbal fight with another neighbour who had recently gone through an operation. The children of the two were playing in the street and started fighting with each other. Well, the neighbour who had recently received surgical treatment complained to the wife of the police officer, who informed her husband. So later the husband complained to the recently operated on neighbour, and my brother found out about it and tried to defend the neighbour. He told the cop not to shout at her because she wasn't even in a condition to leave the house. Well, a couple of days later the policeman beat up my brother to such an extent that he had to go to the hospital. Because we filed a complaint, a couple of days later some police officers went after my brother, and they detained him without further ado and took him to prison. It was like a kidnapping. Like everyone, I think that this man, well, he's more powerful, he abuses the power of his public office.

This example not only offers us a good illustration of how the microcosm of police instrumentalization, conceived as intentional efforts to use the police as a means for achieving security, protection or conflict-related personal goals outside officially sanctioned formal-legal ways, works according to the perceptions of the local residents. It also demonstrates that the same features of the local police force, which were initially perceived by most of the interview partners as threatening and dangerous, are the principal reason why people (and in many cases the same interview partners) relate to them and use them for their private purposes. In particular, the legal faculties and coercive powers of the local police were perceived as important resources for (informally and illegally) resolving a variety of personal problems and conflicts, often by punitive means. It was this privileged access of the police to such resources, derived from the coercive powers of the state, which converted this institution into the single most attractive actor within the local protection business.

However, it is important to stress that such forms of instrumentalizing public security for private purposes are not necessarily examples of informal practices or corruption. Although these informal practices seem to be predominant in such arrangements, there are also possibilities of instrumentalizing the police through formal ways. As a high-ranking member of the Attorney General of the Federal District stated, the excessive workload of her institution is in part also related to the fact that many people, in particular those from marginalized communities, try to convert personal problems into legal problems, frequently on the basis of false accusations, in order to provoke the intervention of the Judicial Police in the hopes that the 'suspect' gets arrested. According to her perception, there is an observable trend that in order to solve personal problems, 'people are increasingly referring to the strongest manifestation of the state, which is the Penal Law'. This development, according to her, was due to the profound *belief* in the efficiency of the Penal Law, which does not so much stem from the impersonal character of the law as a medium of the regulation of social relations, but from the possibility of using the law as a coercive instrument. Although such cases of the micropolitical uses of lawfare were also reported by local residents, they were mostly related to interfamilial conflicts and problems involving people from different neighbourhoods. More public conflicts involving people from different families in the same neighbourhood were in general not brought before the judicial authorities, due to the belief that the judicialization of the conflict (including the possibility of a lawsuit and prison sentence) would only perpetuate the problem and create a permanent tension inside the community (see also above). However, the statement from the member of the Attorney General of the Federal District clearly shows that local residents have discovered penal law as a resource for solving conflicts in their favour, thereby contributing to the punitive turn in local politics 'from below'.

When turning to less punitive and more protection-centred practices, it is a frequent phenomenon that people provide money, free food or drinks to local police officers in order to informally purchase their protection services. As one local shopkeeper stated in this regard, he organized other merchants in his area to collect money to be passed on to the local police officers to keep an eye on their commerce zone and have 'a little bit more surveillance out here'. Such practices of informally contracting policemen for additional protection services are widespread and quite common among many smaller business owners in Mexico City: 'Some of the money goes up the command chain, some down, and the rest remains with the sector chiefs themselves. This amounts to armed protection of private interests by a public institution in exchange for cash payment' (Pansters and Castillo Berthier 2007: 45; see also Anozie et al. 2004: 4).

Such practices 'of armed protection of private interests' are also observable by local residents interested in protecting their homes, cars and other properties. The most common form of such informal police privatization is the illegal 'contracting' of off-duty police officers as informal security guards or *vigilantes*. For example, on the street where I lived during my fieldwork in 2007, nearly every evening two men passed our street in a white car blowing a whistle. When I asked a neighbour about them, I was told that these men were policemen who received a certain amount of money from the local residents to 'keep an eye on our street'. This deal, she said, was organized by some older local residents with good connections to the police. While my neighbour perceived their presence as a good investment in her personal security, another resident explained that she did not feel better protected by them and therefore did not join the group of financial contributors. She furthermore stated that it was common that these presumed policemen were acting in a way that made it difficult to distinguish between protection and extortion. While it seems that many of such informal arrangements benefit all parties involved – the police by providing them with additional income, and the contractors by receiving additional protection – the case of the vigilantes also clearly demonstrates that the dividing line separating voluntary donations from outright extortion can be quite thin.

Another pattern of police privatization is based on informal contacts and deals with local authorities. One local NGO member gave an illustrative example of such forms of cooperation between neighbours and local authorities. She explained that in a central area of Mexico City local residents organized themselves in order to pay for police cars, contributing, as she stated, to a 'privatization of public security'. To this end, 'the neighbours buy the patrol cars [*las patrullas*], and they [the local authorities] send them the officers, of course. [...] Because they pay for the cars, but the cars don't come with the officers. They buy public security in order to protect themselves. That's disgusting, isn't it?'. What makes such informal protection arrangements attractive for local authorities is that, as shown in Chapter 2, many politicians have discovered the political and economic benefits that can be derived by informally providing public services to local residents in search of additional protection. Nevertheless, from the local residents' point of view such politicized forms of police privatization are sometimes perceived as ambiguous blessings, as they can quickly turn into highly politicized protection rackets under the control of politicians and their clientelist networks.

Private security and gated communities

While it is beyond the scope of this section to offer a detailed assessment of private security in Mexico City (on this subject see Alvarado and Davis 2000; Müller 2010b; Reames 2008), a brief description is required to better understand this phenomenon. Private security, for most of the twentieth century, played a rather marginal role within the local security context. This situation changed during the mid-1990s, in large parts as a consequence of the social dislocations that resulted from the 1994 economic crisis and the neoliberalization of Mexico's economy, which contributed to a hitherto unparalleled increase in street crime, in particular between 1994 and 1998 (see Chapter 1). As rising crime levels were related to problems of the local police forces, many residents and businesses started to search for alternative means of protection beyond the state, and Mexico's NAFTA-related economic opening now allowed foreign private security companies to operate in the country, thus offering a commercial solution to these problems.

While the enacting of the 1993 Public Security Law, whose Articles 67–76 defined basic requirements for commercial security provision, clearly anticipated that foreign (as well as national) private security companies would increasingly start operating in Mexico City after NAFTA took effect, the rise of crime and insecurity around 1994 triggered a veritable private security boom in the city. In 1994 alone, the recently created Private Security Services Registration Department counted 2,122 security companies operating in the city. In 2006, there were 507 officially registered private security companies, with some 8,408 employees (SSPDF 2006: 494) working in Mexico City: about one private counterpart for every fourth agent of Mexico City's police force. However, the official private policing market is outmatched by the equally, if not faster, growing informal market for private policing in Mexico City. As the security director of a large Mexican shopping mall chain explained:

> Many [private security] companies are not very professional. These are companies that are also frequently illegal. They don't have the necessary official permission. Their training programs and their armament are not inspected by the authorities and in many cases the businesses contracting their services are not that good as well, like bars, discotheques, etcetera. This is also the reason why they are not interested in higher professional standards. [...] The police in Mexico, public as well as private are perceived as the last employment option. [...] So how do you professionalize these guys when in the majority of cases it is like that; a low quality of instruction, accustomed to acting at the margins of the law, accustomed to benefit from their power and from being armed. How can this be changed? It is very complicated. The problems of private security mirror the problems of public security.

Indeed, many private security providers not only operate beyond the law, they also contribute to the crime problems within the city. Frequently private security companies based in Mexico City, many of them with close connections to the local police, are actively engaged in criminal activities such as drug trafficking, burglary and kidnapping (Mendieta Jiménez 2006: 409–410). To assume that under these circumstances the growth of private security services produces positive spillover effects and contributes to an improvement of the local security situation or the quality of public security, seems to be rather wishful thinking. In fact, for many inhabitants of Mexico City, the presence of security guards in their neighbourhoods hardly evokes the feeling of more protection and security. As one local shopkeeper attested:

> Here they installed a kind of police which is… private security. But they are of no use, nor do they help us. We don't even know who their boss is, or what they do, nothing. They do nothing else than [demand] cash… and you don't know what they are doing with it [the money]. Until now, I don't know if they have any connections with the police. […] I understood that somebody contracted them, but I don't know who. Somebody hired them, brought them here and until now they are still there. Various times they came and asked for money, they give you a ticket and mark you. I don't know if it is so that they see that you cooperated. Since the moment they appeared, I asked about the name of their boss, where they came from, if something happens to me or if I don't like their service, with whom or where I could complain. They never gave me an answer.

This widely observable phenomenon of negative perceptions and experiences with private policing is well captured in the following interview passage from a local middle-class resident: 'I think the private security is not very convenient because what shall one [private] policeman do against five [criminals]. On the contrary, they will scare this guy whom they have sent as a private security [guard]. Against five people he can do nothing.' Furthermore, when asked about the quality of private policing in Mexico City, one security consultant argued that only a very small, high-priced segment of the formal security market specialized in VIP-protection services and resolving kidnappings without police involvement can actually be considered as a protective investment really 'worth the money'.

As argued above, this is closely related to the predominantly informal character of the local security market. The latter, in turn, is not just the outcome of deficient regulatory efforts. It is also related to political calculations. In fact, many politicians, while being aware of the problems of the local market for privatized protection, fear that the strict enforcement of regulatory standards is politically risky, because it might alienate potential voters. As one local politician who participated in the formulation of the current private security law admitted, a stricter regulation of private security companies would certainly be desirable. However, she went on to explain, that legal regulation should not hinder the urban poor from finding employment in the private security sector, as this was one of the most accessible sources of income for those at society's margins. Therefore, a too strict enforcement of existing laws would mean that she herself could have a problem with her electoral base (Müller 2010b: 142–156).

While private security might thus offer employment for marginalized Mexico City residents, in particular for those with little or no education, it also exposes those at the margins of urban society to abusive and violent behaviour. One basic function of private protection in neoliberal Mexico City is the reinforcement of the 'entrenchment of the wealthy in gated communities and de-territorialized security systems which mirror land uses and fragmentary interactions of the North American model' (Canclini 2008: 186). In line with this, the private security boom was accompanied by growing citizen complaints against abuses committed by private security personnel, contributing to this spatial segregation (see Davis 2006: 77). And most victims of such abuses came from the most marginalized segments of urban society, like street children (Müller 2010b: 144–145). In this regard, the boom of private security adds a commercial dimension to the punitive governing of marginality under neoliberalism in the punitive city.

As the above made reference to gated communities indicates, another aspect of privatized and commodified protection in neoliberal Mexico City consists in the proliferation of gated forms of housing. As Villoro has summed it up: 'The democratization of fear provokes that more and more people are living in a condition of partition from the rest of the city' (Villoro 2008: 28). While gated living in Mexico City can be traced back to colonial times, the more recent boom of gated communities is inseparable from the urbanization of neoliberalism and the 'metropolization of crime' that affected the city since the mid-1990s, leading to an 'explosion of walled and gated large apartment complexes' (Low 2005: 3), either through the construction of closed and gated residential complexes (Guerrien 2004; Kanitscheider 2002; Müller 2015) or the closing and gating of already existing residential structures: 'It is in this volatile environment that the wealthier families have begun to gate themselves. First individually, house by house in better neighborhoods, and then in groups of three or four houses on a street' (Low 2005: 9).

Within this process, the walls of gated communities become symbolic and material borders that protect a community of imagined equals from the disturbances and threats of 'outsiders' turned security risks. Thereby the boom of gated communities not only further enhances the already strong pattern of neoliberal spatial segregation, it also leads to a growing securitization of urban space from below.

Like the forms of self-policing mentioned above, this creates an antagonistic space in which those living behind closed gates imagine themselves as being both protected from and threatened by the criminal urban 'other'. And as, the democratization of gated communities in the city, far from being an exclusive upper-class phenomenon has reached the middle and even upper-lower class segments of local society (Villoro 2008: 28), it has exacerbated the securitized dichotomizing of the social in the punitive city. It produces spatially grounded and grounding antagonistic identities that are based on an imagined community of 'us', those living behind the gates, and 'them' living outside. When 'inside' is associated with security and 'outside' symbolizes insecurity, every outsider is a potential security threat against which one must protect and isolate oneself. In this respect, as elsewhere in Latin America, the proliferation of 'fortified enclaves', defined as 'privatized, enclosed, and monitored spaces for residence, consumption, leisure and work', and whose 'central justification is the fear of violent crime' (Caldeira 2000: 213), contributes to the punitiveness of urban society by inscribing a punitive 'us-vs.-them' antagonism deep into the material re-design of urban space in the punitive city.

Indigenous justice

The final dimension of the universe of private protection and punishment in contemporary Mexico City that I will address in this chapter consists of security practices by indigenous communities, ranging from internal social control practices to cases of vigilante justice, including lynchings. The latter, at first sight, seem to be a form of simple retribution. However, in more analytical terms, such practices can be conceived as a form of 'everyday policing' that 'reacts to moral transgressions perceived to threaten the community' (Jensen 2007: 49; see also Baker 2004). Before turning to the acts of moral transgression that contribute to such manifestations of punitive everyday policing in Mexico City neighbourhoods with predominant indigenous populations, some aspects about indigenous communities in Mexico City and their relationship with the public institutions of the administration of justice must be highlighted.

According to the census data from the Mexican National Statistic Institute (Instituto Nacional de Estadística y Geografía INEGI), 118,424 people five years and older speak an indigenous language in Mexico City. However, the real percentage of people with an indigenous background in the capital seems to be much higher as the exclusive focus on language is unable to give a detailed account of the actual size of the indigenous population. In this respect, a study by the Mexican National Commission for the Development of the Indigenous People (CDI) mentioned that about 400,000 indigenous people (about 4 per cent of the total city's population) are living in Mexico City (CDI and PNUD 2006: 79). Despite the granting of substantial formal rights to indigenous communities according to the Law on Indigenous Rights and Culture (approved by the Mexican Congress in 2001) which includes the official recognition of customary, or 'traditional justice' (for an overview of these issues, see Sierra 2005: 53–55), according to a report published by the Human Rights Commission of the Federal District, the local indigenous population suffers disproportionally from high and systematic levels of marginalization (CDHDF 2007: 11).

It is in the realm of policing and the administration of justice that this marginalization is most striking, reflecting both an institutionalized racism as well as abusive police practices aimed at extorting members of indigenous communities (Igreja Lemos 2004: 433–435). As a consequence, the formal justice system might not be the main point of reference for indigenous people when faced with problems of insecurity. In fact, in their efforts to deal with problems of crime and insecurity, many indigenous communities in Mexico City resort to their own legal cultures and notions of justice; practices that are frequently described as 'traditional customs' (*usos y costumbres*; for a critique of such interpretations see Bartra 2007: 160–175). Adapting these 'traditional' legal cultures to a threatening, and insecure neoliberal urban environment permits indigenous communities, characterized by high levels of internal social cohesion, to deal with many security problems without the involvement of public authorities, which are widely perceived as inefficient and abusive. Hence, indigenous communities frequently police themselves and administer their own justice. For example, some forty *triquis* families, coming from the north-eastern part of the State of Oaxaca, settled in a small area in downtown Mexico City. They have created a particular system of norms and social conducts that range from the organization of community work and religious festivities to the administration of justice and policing. They 'keep an eye' on their area and the assembly of families' sanctions transgressions of established community norms and decides how to punish infractions (CDHDF 2007: 42). Such practices are very similar to some of the collective self-policing efforts described above, and in general centre around everyone being vigilant, which permits immediate and collective responses in the case of a crime committed within their community. The following example from the predominantly indigenous neighbourhood of Santa Rosa Xochiac, in the borough of Alvaro Obregón, offers a good description of these practices:

> It is normal that the people take justice into their own hands. Everybody knows each other and if an unknown person appears, that person is immediately detected and observed. When this person is surprised committing a crime, it is apprehended, the people toll the bells, come together and normally give the person a good pounding (*una buena golpiza*) and deliver him to the police. (ProDh 2001: 40–41)

As this case shows, despite the overly negative experiences of indigenous communities with the Mexico City police, it would be wrong to assume that indigenous communities would abandon the official system of the administration of justice. Rather, public institutions are frequently consulted as complementary assistance and in cases of serious crimes, such as rapes or homicides, they seem to remain the central point of reference – notwithstanding overly negative experiences with public policing (Igreja Lemos 2004: 429; Müller 2012c; 2012d). In this regard, indigenous communities in Mexico City, not unlike other parts of the local population, selectively and intentionally decide when and where to turn to formal state institutions and it seems like more serious cases of crime are preferably transferred to the state and its police forces.

Another practice, which is frequently associated with indigenous communities in Mexico City, is that of literally 'taking the law into one's own hands' through acts of vigilante justice; acts which most of all take the form of lynching. Throughout the 1990s, the phenomenon of lynching proliferated throughout Mexico, including Mexico City (Fuentes Díaz 2005; ProDh 2001; Vilas 2001). The most prominent and probably most dramatic case of lynching in Mexico City, and perhaps in the whole country, occurred on 23 November 2004 in the borough of Tláhuac. The victims were three members of the Federal Preventive Police, who were perceived by local residents as 'girl robbers' (*robachicas*). In front of the cameras of Mexican television, two of the police officers were burned alive, while the other was seriously injured (on the Tláhuac lynching, see Uildriks 2010: chapter 1; Azaola 2008: chapter 3).

While the presence of TV cameras contributed to the exceptional attention that the Tláhuac case received by local and international commentators, lynching has been a quite frequent occurrence in contemporary Mexico City. As one study that analysed the distribution of lynchings in Mexico for the period between 1985 and 2005 concluded: 'The Federal District and its neighbouring urban communities [*zonas conurbanas*] represent the highest concentration of lynchings (64), due to its population density. It is followed by Chiapas (41), Oaxaca (36), the State of México (32), Puebla (24) and Morelos (21)' (Ramírez Cuevas 2005: 2). A report on the situation in Mexico City, published by the Office of the Attorney General, stated that between December 2004 and February 2005, twenty-three cases of lynching were reported to the Attorney General of the Federal District. Most of these cases happened in the rural-peripheral parts of

Mexico City (*La Reforma* 2005), areas with a very high concentration of indigenous communities. In light of this, it becomes understandable that lynching in Mexico City is frequently presented as the quasi-logical consequence of the existence and dominance of traditional value systems and ideas of indigenous justice, the so-called *usos y costumbres* (ProDh 2001: 40–41; Vilas 2001).

Although this explanation seemingly can account for the overwhelming concentration of lynchings in areas with a predominant indigenous population, it can be criticized for oversimplifying the underlying social causes of these lynchings. Rather than expressing the persistence of seemingly traditional practices, the striking incidence of lynching in such areas also reflects the erosion of social cohesion and the weakening of the power of local authorities as a consequence of recent neoliberal economic and urban developments that have further marginalized these areas (Pansters and Castillo Berthier 2007: 52; Ramírez Cuevas 2004). Additionally, most communities where lynchings have taken place in recent years are also suffering from high levels of socio-economic and political marginalization, as well as a very deficient state infrastructure, including the realm of policing where in general, 'the state's institutions fail to attend the needs of large sectors of the population' (Focus 21/2004: 7).

However, it would be wrong to suggest that such forms of 'taking justice into one's own hands' are beyond the state. First, as could already be observed in the aforementioned case of Santa Rosa Xochiac, most acts of vigilante justice end up with the criminals being handed over to the *public* authorities (*Reforma* 13 February 2005). In addition to this material state presence, there is also a more symbolic aspect of state–society interactions involved. As Goldstein has convincingly demonstrated in his ethnographic account of lynching in Cochabamba, Bolivia, such punishments serve a double purpose:

> Through such violent practices, the politically marginalized find an avenue for the communication of grievances against the inadequacies of the state's legal order, while at the same time deploying the rhetoric of justice and law to police their communities against crime. (Goldstein 2003: 23)

In other words, lynching is not just a form of indigenous punishment 'beyond the state'. Rather, it represents a symbolic action that presupposes state power, communicates with it and, ultimately, reproduces it (Goldstein 2003: 25; see also Goldstein 2004). These findings can also be applied to lynchings in Mexico City. Owing to the fact that the victims in the Tláhuac case, which captured nearly all of the academic and media attention when it comes to lynchings in Mexico City, were policemen should not conceal the hidden communicative gestures and underlying symbolic negotiation of state–society relations that took place in and through this event, and whose symbolic subtext also expressed 'a desire for protection under the law' and a 'call for improved police protection' (Goldstein 2004: 198).

Lynching, and vigilante justice by indigenous communities can thus be described as an expression of neoliberal violence: 'Neoliberal violence is at once structural and undeniably physical; it entails an inequitable distribution of resources within a rigidly hierarchical society, which ultimately must be implemented and maintained by state violence, and which in turn engenders violent responses' (Goldstein 2005: 390). On a structural level, these practices reflect, as shown above, the increasing marginalization of poor urban communities in general, and of those with a high percentage of indigenous residents in particular, which is clearly visible in the lack of adequate security provision by the state. But these practices also reflect the ultimate consequences of neoliberalism's call for citizens' responsibility to take care of their own life. In literally taking law and punishment into their own hands, marginalized communities respond to neoliberalism's ideology of self-responsibilization, which in the realm of security governance often translates into discourses about community policing or community participation (see Chapter 2), by resisting their marginalization through the use of forms of bottom-up communal punishment that serve as symbolic communication efforts to press for more state protection. In other words, such forms of vigilante justice reflect 'a fully modern response to insecurity, reflecting the very logic of neoliberal democracy that requires individual responsibility for self-preservation, without reliance on the state' (Arias and Goldstein 2010b: 22). In doing so, however, citizens further contribute to, rather than undermine, the deepening of neoliberal self-responsibilization and the punitive re-making of urban politics in Mexico City by adding another layer to the micro-level universe of punitive and penalizing non-state practices in the city.

Conclusion

This chapter analysed the multiple bottom-up efforts by Mexico City residents to search for more protection in an insecure urban environment. While such bottom-up efforts are often perceived as *the* solution to urban security problems, as can be seen, for instance, in the promotion of community policing or citizen security programmes and discourses in Mexico as well as elsewhere in Latin America, by NGOs, governments, international donors and academics (see Chapter 4), the findings presented in this chapter caution against an uncritical embrace of the empowering and democratic potentials of such efforts. It was demonstrated that such bottom-up responses to insecurity, ranging from different forms of self-policing and community justice to the informal as well as formal commodification of protection, reinforce those top-down punitive efforts that, as shown throughout the book, during the last decade transformed Mexico City into a punitive city. Be it through the construction of us-vs.-them identities that reproduce penal populism's antagonizing logics of a 'threatened' us and a criminal 'other' at the neighbourhood level, the contracting of security guards, coercive bribery and the related appropriation of police forces for private (punitive) purposes, the micropolitical resort to lawfare, or by taking the law literally into one's own hands, Mexico City residents, in their efforts to deal with neoliberal violence, are active agents of the punitive transformation of local politics.

This feeds into the broader conclusion of this book; that in contrast to the dominant *policía comunitaria* and *seguridad ciudadana* discourses, improving the local security situation is not so much about making security governance more local. Nor is it about bringing it closer to citizens and/or communities. In order to avoid that community policing and related efforts contribute to the creation of veritable *police communities* that become de facto proxies of punitive neoliberal state makers, a desecuritization of local politics is needed.

CONCLUSION

This book has assessed the causes and consequences of the punitive turn in Mexico City that, during the last decade, has transformed the city into a punitive city in which those at society's margins are increasingly confronted with a penalizing and criminalizing mode of neoliberal governance of marginality (Wacquant 2009a). This development, as argued in the introduction, is not exclusive to Mexico City. Rather, throughout Latin America, and largely irrespective of the political orientations of local and national governments, a punitive turn can be identified. This is most visible in a hitherto unparalleled increase in the region's inmate populations and the increasing centrality of punitive politics in the governing of Latin American societies (e.g. Hathazy and Müller 2016; Müller 2012a; Schild 2015; Wacquant 2008a).

Analysing these developments from the vantage point of Mexico City, a context that in a paradigmatic way illustrates the transformation of urban spaces into punitive spaces, thus allows drawing some broader conclusions regarding the causes and consequences of the recent punitive transformations observable in many Latin American cities, as well as offering some analytical counterpoints that might potentially open up the highly securitized debates on the future of Latin American cities beyond their predominant focus on police, criminals and prisons.

Regarding the causes of the transformation of Mexico City into a punitive city, the book has demonstrated that this process is inseparable from the urbanization of neoliberalism, the repercussions of the local democratization process and the political re-working of security issues. Regarding more structural features of this development, neoliberalism's 'going urban' in Mexico City contributed to a deindustrialization of the city's economy, accompanied by a hitherto unparalleled informalization of the local job market and the emergence of 'new illegalities' (Aguiar 2012). Participating in the latter – from drug trafficking to the re-sale of stolen goods, to the engagement in product piracy – has become an increasingly important economic survival strategy for those at urban society's margins who are trying to make a living in the informal economy and struggling with the related socio-economic hardship and lack of social protection, which, in turn, worsen against the backdrop of their 'forced entrepreneurialism' (Portes and Roberts 2005).

As in other places affected by neoliberal transformation processes, the Mexico City administrations of the leftist PRD, from the late-1990s onwards, responded to this situation 'by engaging in short-termist forms of interspatial competition, place-marketing, and regulatory undercutting in order to attract investment and jobs' (Brenner and Theodore 2002: 20). The resulting interiorization of neoliberalism produced new, Global City-oriented, forms of 'property development schemes, business-incubator projects, new strategies of social control, policing, and surveillance' (ibid.: 21), in order to sell and promote Mexico City as a safe and attractive investment location. The overall consequence of this has been that the democratically elected PRD governments implemented repressive policing strategies targeting the city's urban 'undesirables' that are not too different from those policing efforts associated with the seven decades of Mexican authoritarianism under PRI rule. Thus, democratic Mexico City shows a remarkable continuity with its authoritarian predecessor, in particular because the PRD's vision of urban governance came to emphasize security instead of freedom. The resulting punitive governing of marginality in the city increasingly excludes the most marginalized segments of the urban population whose lives the local democratization process was expected to improve.

As shown in this book, most of these efforts focused on the historic downtown area which became a veritable laboratory for the punitive makeover of urban politics. It was here, where new crime prevention approaches and lawfare tools, which convert the rule of law into rule through law, were first tested. This came with the focus on the regulation of undesirable behaviour in public spaces in order to create and preserve the safety and economic potential of commodified urban spaces, and manifested in new expansive security governance schemes, from the application of zero tolerance policing to the enacting of the LCC. As the test results have been integrated into city-wide policing efforts and legal-regulatory frameworks, it can be said that the neoliberal urban renewal project in downtown Mexico City has been *the* driving force behind the transformation of the city into a punitive city.

However, the book also demonstrated that the punitive re-making of urban governance in Mexico City cannot exclusively be attributed to the impersonal workings of neoliberal market forces and their penalizing consequences that produce new forms of punitive exclusion, marginalization and inequality. As Angotti reminds us, the 'production and reproduction of urban inequalities is not simply a product of an unequal system. It has a life of its own and involves the conscious and sometimes creative intervention of individuals and social groups' (Angotti 2013b: 11).

This brings in the local democratization process. In fact, as this book demonstrated, the democratization of local politics since the 1990s, leading to the first elections of the local mayor in 1997 and the rise of the PRD as the dominant political force in the city, substantially contributed to the punitive turn in local politics. Three factors are central in this regard. First of all, and most importantly for understanding the multiple constraints parties are confronted with when trying to politically navigate on the terrain of urban neoliberalism, the Mexico City democratization process was embedded within wider political transformations of the Mexican political system. Since the PRD established its power in Mexico City, all local administrations have been confronted with either PRI or PAN presidents at the national level, where, according to Mexico's federal system, many of the city's spending priorities and federal fiscal transfers are determined (frequently discretionary). These national actors, following basic political reasoning, have little interest in improving the local mayor's economic and political performance – and financial resources – as they are fearful that such a success could be converted into political capital. Thus, the embrace of a neoliberal urban development strategy and the related securitization of urban space were to a large extent driven by the local governments' needs of expanding their own revenue-generating capacity and the related decision to opt for a neoliberal Global City-oriented urban development strategy.

A second, and related, aspect that explains why a leftist party like the PRD has been an active driving force behind the transformation of Mexico City into a punitive city is related to the symbolic relevance of the nation's capital for the wider political aspirations of local politicians. In this regard, the PRD has used its urban policies in Mexico City for improving and 'selling' its image as a party capable of governing the country's most important city in order to enhance its political position on the national level. As Wigle has argued in this regard, Mexico City 'represents both an important political base for the PRD and a policy showcase for its broader political ambitions in Mexico' (Wigle 2014: 575). When considering Mexico's current security crisis, it is obvious that a good political performance on the security front is important political capital for the larger national ambitions of the PRD leadership. Moreover, as the metropolization of crime also elevated insecurity to 'the single-most relevant issue on the urban agenda' in Mexico City (Castillo 2008: 181), it is not surprising that, in the end, the pressure confronted by the PRD to demonstrate that it can secure the city has made the party adopt policing and lawfare approaches that are similar to those implemented at the national level, notwithstanding the PRD's discursive commitment to social questions.

However, the punitive transformation of urban governance in Mexico City is not just an elite project. A third factor that explains the political dimension of the making of the punitive city in relation to the local democratization process stems from bottom-up responses to crime and insecurity as well as related political pressures from the electorate to confront them. In this regard, the book's findings demonstrate that the local electorate has, in general, rewarded the PRD's punitive agenda, including the resort to penal populism, by allowing the party to stay in power for nearly two decades. Moreover, as evidenced by the spread of gated communities, private security, multiple forms of self-policing and community justice, bottom-up responses to urban insecurity fed into and exacerbated the overall punitive turn in local politics. In the guise of what could be called a form of neoliberal grassroots punitivism, bottom-up responses to insecurity, as shown in this book, often tend to divide up the social space into us-vs.-them identities that reproduce penal populism's antagonizing logics of a 'threatened' us and a criminal 'other' at the neighbourhood level. Far from making security provision more inclusive and democratic, as many proponents of such bottom-up and community-centred approaches to urban security governance suggest, the findings presented in this book caution against an uncritical embrace of bottom-up efforts that too often is blind to the resulting exclusionary, power-laden and punitive consequences. To put it in other terms, just because it is 'bottom-up', doesn't make it good.

The problems with bottom-up security and protection efforts in Mexico City are also related to the embeddedness of the punitive turn in local urban governance within established informal political structures and practices, notably political clientelism. Far from being erased during the democratization process, as many democracy promoters hoped for, clientelism has demonstrated remarkable resilience and even expanded into the realm of security provision, allowing for informal access to public security that de facto privatizes state protection and coercion. Moreover, while such informal practices also sometimes allow for the contestation and mediation of penalizing state projects, the flipside of this outcome is that the overall punitiveness of urban governance even made the most marginalized segments of the city's growing informal economy increasingly dependent upon protection from political bosses and brokers in order to negotiate over the non-enforcement of penalizing laws in their favour, thereby expanding punitive exclusion into the realm of informal politics where those outside clientelist networks are the ones who suffer most from the penalizing consequences of neoliberal law enforcement in the city.

Similar, and at first sight puzzling, findings, at least for those who assume that civic activism, the incorporation of international security best practice, as well as knowledge produced and disseminated by NGOs, is the perfect way of improving and democratizing urban security in Latin America, relate to the fact that the vernacularization of international policing best practices, such as zero tolerance, community policing or citizen security approaches are highly compatible with, and partly responsible for, the punitive turn in local politics. Moreover, NGOs, the darlings of most international donors, aid workers and academics, also contributed to this outcome by legitimizing and selling such best practice in a depoliticizing fashion that risks perpetuating rather than transforming the insecurity-related status quo, while improving the organizations' standing and position within an increasingly competitive securocratic NGO marketplace.

In this regard, the overall findings of this book clearly demonstrate that the violence affecting contemporary Latin America 'is not the simple result of institutional failure but the logical outcome of neoliberal democracy's unfolding' that has been accompanied by 'widening income inequalities and mounting poverty across the region' (Arias and Goldstein 2010b: 16). The in-depth assessment of the transformation of Mexico City into a punitive city provides ample evidence for this sobering assessment, in particular by demonstrating that in neoliberalism's 'securitized democracies' (Pearce 2010), the punitive violence inherent in the region's urban democratic orders is actively co-produced. It is the outcome of top-down efforts of reordering social relations by punitive politics and bottom-up responses to confront the resulting forms of 'neoliberal violence(s)' in order to have a more secure and protected everyday that is threatened by the physical and structural violence brought about by the neoliberal transformations of city spaces.

If standard responses such as civic activism, community engagement, the vernacularization of international best practices or the transnationalization of security governance, not to mention more standard efforts such as institutional police reform (on this issue, see Müller 2012c; Uildriks 2010) did not improve the local security situation, we are left with the puzzling question of what now?

Without claiming to offer a comprehensive answer to this question, nor to come up with a solution, my response to this question would be that more than ten years of researching questions of insecurity, policing and violence in Mexico City often left me puzzled regarding the taken-for-grantedness and apparent self-explanatory character the word 'security' has acquired among local residents, journalists politicians, bureaucrats and academics, including myself. However, one only has to look back twenty-five years or so to see that the topic of security, for most academics, journalists and Mexicans was literally a non-topic. This is not to say that Mexico was peaceful and non-violent. In fact, violence and coercion were central pillars of the post-revolutionary Mexican state (see Pansters 2012b). However, the socialization and perverse democratization of violence that contemporary Mexico is facing was unimaginable for most of the twentieth century. And the coincidence of the contemporary timeliness of violence and (in) security, as well as the resulting punitiveness, put on the local political agenda with the rolling-out of neoliberalism and democratization is more than just a coincidence. As this book has demonstrated, these processes are inseparable from efforts of implementing, protecting and enforcing a neoliberal vision of urban order that often, because of the underlying and resulting structural violence, transforms citizens' responses to neoliberal violence and their everyday search for security and protection into proxy powers that deepen the punitive transformation of the city.

The problem with, and political potential of, security is that it is a relational concept. It always depends upon its other, which is insecurity, and the social groups that can be framed by law, in public debates and academic publications as a threat or risk. In this regard, security is not in and of itself a neutral category. It is 'not some kind of universal or transcendental value', rather it is 'a mode of governing, a political technology through which individuals, groups, classes, and, ultimately modern capital is reshaped and ordered' (Neocleous 2008: 4). The latter point is particularly important as much of the neutral, in fact, technocratic knowledge produced and disseminated on security in urban Latin America is (often deliberately and conveniently) blind to the political dimension of a mode of governing that in practice hardly lives up to conceptual ideas and ideals of a public good (see Müller 2013a). In this regard, a partial and provisional answer to the 'what now?' question might consist in a call for a desecuritization of political and academic discourse on urban governance in Latin America, and stress the need for an alternative research agenda that, by embedding the question of (in)security within a broader inter-disciplinary political-economy analytical framework, might be able to identify alternative responses towards urban violence that by moving beyond the 'police and criminals' narrative could possibly challenge the ongoing criminalization of urban marginality and the growing punitiveness of cities throughout the region.

This should not be read as an abstract academic call for critical self-reflection regarding our unintended complicity in these processes. There are indeed very concrete needs for more security and protection in cities like Mexico City. Most people I met and talked to, in fact, felt constrained by an all-pervasive climate of fear, most visible in the multiple forms of self-policing observed in Chapter 4. However, in light of the findings presented in this book – and the more than sobering accounts of more than twenty years of police reform in the city – thinking about decentring and desecuritizing security debates might be worthwhile, as the solution to the local insecurity problems might not be found in more police, more 'going local', the vernacu-larization of international best practices or new laws. As Diane Davis argued nearly a decade ago:

> Forget democratic deepening; forget bettering the quality of democracy; forget the nuts and bolts of police reform. How about reconstructing, reviving, or renewing modern enlighten-ment ideals and an attendant commitment to the rule of law with the hope that with such social infrastructure a vibrant democracy will once again become something worth struggling for? (Davis 2006: 82)

A decade after this call, and against the background of the rule through law-related punitive turn in local politics, the 'attendant commitment to the rule of law' might be more complicated and ambivalent than she might have thought. However, her emphasis on struggling for a social infrastructure that allows for the emergence of a vibrant and not punitive democracy is as urgent as it was ten years ago. It might be through such political struggles rather than through apolitical and penalizing securocratic experiments that Mexico City's security situation will be improved in an inclusive and democratic, not punitive, way. While this, as Davis reminds us, might be the hardest of all possible transitions to achieve, 'yet it surely will be the most lasting and worthwhile' (ibid.).

In leaving it at that, I want to end this book not with a definite statement, argument or answer that would settle the debates on insecurity in Mexico City. Rather, I hope that this conclusion and the evidence presented in this book will inspire questions and new ways of engaging with the question of urban security that, by desecuritizing this topic might contribute to move related discourses and practices out of the punitive one-way street that has become the dominant pattern of neoliberal urban governance in Mexico City and most other urban spaces in contemporary Latin America.

REFERENCES

Aguiar, J. C. G. (2012) 'Policing New Illegalities: Piracy, Raids, and Madrinas', in W. Pansters (ed.), *Violence, Coercion, and State-Making in Twentieth-Century Mexico. The Other Half of the Centaur*, Palo Alto, CA: Stanford University Press, pp. 159–181.

Aitken, R., N. Craske, G. A. Jones, and D. E. Stansfield (eds) (1996) *Dismantling the Mexican State?* Basingstoke: Palgrave Macmillan.

Alba Vega, C. (2010) 'Regulación social y violencia en el mundo de la economía informal. El caso del centro histórico de la cuidad de México.' Paper presented at the 'Ateliê de pesquisas: llegalismos, cidade e política: Perspectivas comparativas quatro metrópoles latino-americanas,' Universidade de São Paulo, 23–24 February 2010.

Alvarado, A. and D. E. Davis (2000) 'Banking Security in Mexico City: Mixing Public and Private Police', in The Vera Institute of Justice (ed.) *The Public Accountability of Private Police – Lessons from New York, Johannesburg and México City*, New York: Vera Institute of Justice, pp. 34–45.

Amar, P. (2013) *The Security Archipelago. Human-Security States, Sexuality Politics, and the End of Neoliberalism*, Durham, NC: Duke University Press.

Angotti, T. (2013a) *The New Century of the Metropolis: Urban Enclaves and Orientalism*, New York, NY: Routledge.

Angotti, T. (2013b) 'Urban Latin America: Violence, Enclaves, and Struggles for Land', *Latin American Perspectives*, 40(2): 5–20.

Anozie, V., J. Shinn, K. Skarlatos, and J. Urzua (2004) 'Reducing Incentives for Corruption in the Mexico City Police Force.' International Workshop, Public Affairs 869, www.lafollette.wisc.edu/publications/workshops/2003-2004/pa869/2004-MEXICO.pdf [accessed 12 January 2007].

Ansell, A. and K. Mitchell (2010) 'Models of Clientelism and Policy Change: The Case of Conditional Cash Transfer Programmes in Mexico and Brazil', *Bulletin of Latin American Research*, 30(3): 298–312.

Antillano, A., I. Pojomovsky, V. Zubillaga, C. Sepúlveda and R. Hanson (2016) 'The Venezuelan Prison: From Neoliberalism to the Bolivarian Revolution', *Crime, Law and Social Change*, 65(3): 195-211.

Arias, E. D. (2006) *Drugs and Democracy in Rio de Janeiro: Trafficking, Social Networks and Public Security*, Chapel Hill. NC: University of North Carolina Press.

Arias, E. D. and D. M. Goldstein (eds) (2010a) *Violent Democracies in Latin America*, Durham, NC: Duke University Press.

Arias, E. D. and D. M. Goldstein (2010b) 'Violent Pluralism. Understanding the New Democracies of Latin America', in E. D. Arias and D. E. Goldstein (eds), *Violent Democracies in Latin America*, Durham, NC: Duke University Press, pp. 1–33.

Arteaga Botello, N. (2004) *En busca de la legitimidad: Seguridad pública y populismo punitivo en México, 1990-2000*, Mexico City: UACM.

Arteaga, Botello, N. (2013) 'Urban Securitization in Mexico City: A New Public Order?', in R. K. Lippert and K. Walby (eds), *Policing Cities. Urban Securitization and Regulation in a Twenty-First Century World*, Abingdon: Routledge, pp. 231–245.

Atkinson, R. and G. Bridge (2005) 'Introduction', in R. Atkinson and G. Bridge (eds), *Gentrification in a Global Context: The New Urban Colonialism*, London: Routledge, pp. 1–17.

Auyero, J. (2004) *Clientelismo político: Las caras ocultas*, Buenos Aires: Capital Intelectual.

Auyero, J. (2007) *Routine Politics and Violence in Argentina: The Gray Zone of State Power*, Cambridge: Cambridge University Press.

Auyero, J. (2012) *Patients of the State: The Politics of Waiting in Argentina*, Durham, NC: Duke University Press.

Azaola, E. (2008) *Crimen, castigo y violencias en México*. Quito: FLACSO – MDMQ.

Azaola, E. and M. A. Ruiz Torres (2011) 'Poder y abusos de poder entre la Policía Judicial de la Ciudad de México', *Iberoamericana*, 11(41): 99–115.

Azaola, E. and M. Bergman (2007) 'The Mexican Prison System', in W. A. Cornelius and D. A. Shirk (eds), *Reforming the Administration of Justice in Mexico*, Notre Dame, IN: University of Notre Dame Press, pp. 91–114.

Baena Paz, G. and G. G. Saavedra Andrade (2004) 'Entre tribus y jefes: el futuro del PRD en el 2006', en F. R. Vázquez (ed.), *Partido de la Revolución Democrática. Los problemas de la institucionalización*, Mexico City: UNAM-Gernika, pp. 217–259.

Baker, B. (2004) 'Multi-choice Policing in Africa: Is the Continent Following the South African Pattern?' *Society in Transition*, 35(2): 204–223.

Barder, Alexander, D. (2013) 'American Hegemony Comes Home: The Chilean Laboratory and the Neoliberalization of the United States', *Alternatives. Global, Local, Political*, 38(2): 103–121.

Bartra, R. (1999) *Agrarian Structure and Political Power in Mexico*, Baltimore, MD: Johns Hopkins University Press.

Bartra, R. (2007) *Fango sobre la democracia. Textos polémicos sobre la transición Mexicana*, Mexico City: Planeta Mexicana.

Becerra Sánchez, M. (2007) 'Factores asociados a la percepción de la inseguridad pública en el Distrito Federal', in L. González Placancia, J. L. Arce Aguilar and M. Álvarez (eds), *Aproximaciones empíricas al estudio de la inseguridad. Once estudios en materia de seguridad ciudadana en México*, Mexico City: Miguel Ángel Porrua: 105–35.

Becker, A. and M.-M. Müller (2011) 'Null Toleranz für Straßenprostitution? Altstadtaufwertung und die Kriminalisierung "unerwünschter" informeller Ersatzökonomien in Mexiko Stadt', in Alfaro P. d'Alençon, W. A. Imilan and L. M. Sánchez (eds), *Lateinamerikanische Städte im Wandel. Zwischen lokaler Stadtgesellschaft und globalem Einfluss*, Berlin: LIT Verlag, pp. 61–70.

Becker, A. and M.-M. Müller (2013) 'The Securitization of Urban Space and the "Rescue" of Downtown Mexico City: Vision and Practice', *Latin American Perspectives*, 40(2): 77–94.

Beckett, K. (1999) *Making Crime Pay: Law and Order in Contemporary American Politics*, Oxford: Oxford University Press.

Belina, B. and G. Helms (2003) 'Zero Tolerance for the Industrial Past and Other Threats: Policing and Urban Entrepreneurialism in Britain and Germany', *Urban Studies*, 40(9): 1845–1867.

Bergman, M., E. Azaola and A. L. Magaloni (2006) *Delincuencia, marginalidad y desempeño institucional*, Mexico City: CIDE.

Berling, T. V. and C. Bueger (2015) 'Security Expertise: An Introduction', in Berling, T. V. and C. Bueger (eds), *Security Expertise. Practice, Power, Responsibility*, London: Routledge, pp. 1–19.

Bigo, D. (2011) 'Pierre Bourdieu and International Relations: Power of Practices, Practices of Power', *International Political Sociology*, 5(3): 225–258.

Bigo, D. and A. Tsoukala (2008) 'Understanding (In)Security', in D. Bigo and A. Tsoukala (eds), *Terror, Insecurity and Liberty. Illiberal Practices of Liberal Regimes after 9/11*, London: Routledge, pp. 1–9.

Bird, R. and E. Slack (2008) 'Fiscal Aspects of Metropolitan Governance', in E. Rojas, J. R. Cuadrado-Roura and J. M. Fernández Güell (eds), *Governing the Metropolis. Principles and Cases*, Washington, DC: Inter-American Development Bank, pp. 193–259.

Bourdieu, P. (1990) *The Logic of Practice*, Palo Alto CA: Stanford University Press.

Bourdieu, P. (1991) *Language & Symbolic Power*, Oxford: Polity Press.

Bourdieu, P. (1993) *The Field of Cultural Production: Essays on Art and Literature*, Oxford: Polity Press.

Bourdieu, P. and L. Wacquant (1992) *An Invitation to Reflexive Sociology*, Chicago, IL: University of Chicago Press.

Brenner, N. and N. Theodore (2002) 'Cities and the Geographies of "Actually Existing Neoliberalism"', *Antipode*, 33(3): 349–379.

Brock, N. (2008) 'Tepito mala fama', in A. Becker, O. Burkert, A. Doose, A. Jachnow and M. Poppitz (eds), *Verhandlungssache Mexiko Stadt. Umkämpfte Räume, Stadtaneignungen, imaginarios urbanos*, Berlin: b_books, pp. 205–221.

Burbach, R., M. Fox and F. Fuentes (2013) *Latin America's Turbulent Transitions. The Future of Twenty-First Century Socialism*, London: Zed Books.

Buzan, B. and L. Hansen (2009) *The Evolution of International Security Studies*, Cambridge, MA: Cambridge University Press.

Buzan, B., Wæver, O. and J. de Wilde (1998) *Security. A New Framework for Analysis*, Boulder, CO: Lynne Rienner.

Caldeira, T. (2006) '"I Came to Sabotage Your Reasoning" Violence and Resignification of Justice in Brazil', in J. Comaroff and J. Comaroff (eds), *Law and Disorder in the Postcolony*, Chicago, IL: Chicago University Press, pp. 102–148.

Caldeira, T. P. R. (2000) *City of Walls: Crime Segregation, and Citizenship in São Paulo*, Berkeley, CA: University of California Press.

Campesi, G. (2010) 'Policing, Urban Poverty and Insecurity in Latin America: the case of Mexico City and Buenos Aires', *Theoretical Criminology*, 14(4): 447–471.

Canclini, N. (2008) 'Makeshift Globalization', in R. Burdett and D. Sudjic (eds) *The Endless City*, London: Phaidon: 186–190.

Castillo Berthier, H. and G. A. Jones (2009) 'Mean Streets: Youth, Violence, and Daily Life in Mexico City', in G. A. Jones and D. Rodgers (eds), *Youth Violence in Latin America. Gangs and Juvenile Justice in Perspective*, Basingstoke: Palgrave Macmillan, pp. 182–202.

Castillo Olea, J. M. (2006) *The Informal Economy as a Way of Life*. Available at: https://lsecities.net/media/objects/articles/mexico-city-the-informal-economy-as-a-way-of-life/en-gb/ [accessed 18 July 2012].

Castillo, J. (2008) 'After the Explosion', in R. Burdett and D. Sudjic (eds), *The Endless City*, London: Phaidon, pp. 174–185.

Castro Nieto, G. G. (1990) 'Intermediarismo político y sector informal: el comercio ambulante en Tepito', *Nueva Antropología* 11(37): 59–69.

CCE/CESPEDES (Consejo Coordinador Empresarial/Centro de Estudios del Sector Privado para el Desarrollo Sustentable) (2001) *Centro Histórico. Revitalización: Desafío estrategico para el Distrito Federal*, Mexico City: CESPEDES.

CDHDF (Comisión de Derechos Humanos del Distrito Federal) (2001) *Recomendación 3/2001*. Available at: www.cdhdf.org.mx/index.php/recomendaciones/por-ano/2001 [accessed 22 August 2012].

CDHDF (Comisión de Derechos Humanos del Distrito Federal) (2005) *Informe especial sobre la situación de los juzgados cívicos del Distrito Federal durante el 2004*, Mexico City: CDHDF.

CDHDF (Comisión de Derechos Humanos del Distrito Federal) (2007) 'Informe Especial sobre los Derechos de las Comunidades Indígenas Residentes en la Ciudad de México, 2006–2007'. Mexico City: CDHDF.

CDHDF (Comisión de Derechos Humanos del Distrito Federal) (2011) *Informe especial sobre el derecho a la salud de las personas privadas de la libertad en los centros de reclusión en el Distrito Federal 2010-2011*, Mexico City: CDHDF.

CDI (Comisión Nacional para el Desarrollo de los Pueblos Indígenas) and PNUD (Programa de las Naciones Unidas para el Desarrollo) (2006) 'Informe sobre desarrollo humano de los pueblos indígenas de México 2006'. Mexico City: CDI.

Chatterjee, P. (2004) *The Politics of the Governed. Reflections on Popular Politics in Most of the World*, New York: Columbia University Press.

Chevigny, P. (2003) 'The Populism of Fear: Politics of Crime in the Americas', *Punishment and Society*, 5(1): 77–96.

Chodor, T. (2015) *Neoliberal Hegemony and the Pink Tide in Latin America. Breaking up with TINA?*, Basingstoke: Palgrave Macmillan.

Choudry, A. and D. Kapoor (eds) (2013) *NGOization: Complicity, Contradictions and Prospects*, London: Zed Books.

CJSL (Consejería Jurídica y de Servicios Legales) (2011) *V Informe de actividades 2010-1011*, Mexico City: CJSL.

Cobilt Cruz, E. C. (2008) 'Entre el cliente y el patrón: la intermediación política en los periodos de latencia', *Master's Thesis*, México: Flacso México.

Cohen, S. (1979) 'The Punitive City: Notes on the Dispersal of Social Control', *Contemporary Crisis*, 3(4): 339–363.

Collier, S. J. and A. Ong (2005) 'Global Assemblages, Anthropological Problems', in A. Ong and S. J. Collier (eds) *Global Assemblages. Technology, Politics, and Ethics as Anthropological Problems*, Malden, MA: Blackwell, pp. 3–21.

Comaroff, J. and J. Comaroff (2006) 'Law and Disorder in the Postcolony: An Introduction', in J. Comaroff and J. Comaroff (eds), *Law and Disorder in the Postcolony*, Chicago, IL: Chicago University Press, pp. 1–56.

Cornelius, W. A. (1975) *Politics and the Migrant Poor in Mexico City*, Palo Alto CA: Stanford University Press.

Cornelius, W. A. (1999) 'Subnational Politics and Democratization: Tensions between Center and Periphery in the Mexican Political System', in W. A. Cornelius, T. A. Eisenstadt and J. Hindley (eds), *Subnational Politics and Democratization in Mexico*, La Jolla, CA: Center for U.S.–Mexican Studies.

Coulomb, R. (2000) 'El Centro Histórico de la Ciudad de México', in G. Garza (ed.), *La Ciudad de México al fin del segundo milenio*, Mexico City: Gobierno del Distrito Federal, Colegio de México, pp. 530–537.

Cross, J. (1998) *Informal Politics. State and Street Vendors in Mexico City*, Palo Alto CA: Stanford University Press.

Cross, J. (2007) 'Pirates on the High Street: The Streets as a Site Of Local Resistance to Globalization', in J. Cross and A. Morales (eds), *Street Entrepreneurs. People, Place and Politics in Local and Global Perspective*, London: Routledge, pp. 125–144.

Crossa, V. (2009) 'Resisting the Entrepreneurial City: Street Vendors' Struggle in Mexico City's Historic Center', *International Journal of Urban and Regional Research*, 33(1): 43–63.

Dammert, L. and L. Zúñiga (2008) *Prisons: Problems and Challenges for the Americas*, Santiago de Chile, Chile: Flacso.

Davenport, C. (2007a) *State Repression and the Domestic Democratic Peace*, New York: Cambridge University Press.

Davenport, C. (2007b) 'State Repression and Political Order', *Annual Review of Political Science*, 10: 1–23.

Davis, D. E. (1994) *Urban Leviathan. Mexico City in the Twentieth Century*, Temple, PA: Temple University Press.

Davis, D. E. (2006) 'Undermining the Rule of Law: Democratization and the Dark Side of Police Reform in Mexico', *Latin American Politics and Society*, 48(1): 55–86.

Davis, D. E. (2008) 'Insecure Cities: Towards a Reclassification of World Cities in a Global Area', *MIT International Review*, Spring 2008: 31–41.

Davis, D. E. (2010) 'The Political and Economic Origins of Violence and Insecurity in Contemporary Latin America: Past Trajectories and Future Prospects', in E. D. Arias and D. M. Goldstein (eds), *Violent Democracies in Latin America*, Durham, NC: Duke University Press: 35–62.

Davis, D. E. (2013) 'Zero-tolerance Policing, Stealth Real Estate Development, and the Transformation of Public Space: Evidence from Mexico City', *Latin American Perspectives*, 40(2): 53–76.

Davis, D. E. (2015) 'Socio-Spatial Inequality and Violence in Cities of the Global South: Evidence from Latin America', in F. Miraftab, D. Wilson and K. Salo (eds), *Cities and Inequalities in a Global and Neoliberal World*, Abingdon: Routledge, pp. 75–91.

Davis, D. E. and A. Alvarado (2004) 'Mexico City: The Challenge of Political Transition', in D. Chavez and B. Goldfrank (eds), *The Left in the City. Participatory Local Governments in Latin America*, London: Latin American Bureau and TNI, pp. 135–168.

Davis, D. E. and G. Ruiz de Teresa (2013) 'Rescaling Security Strategies. State Tactics and Citizen Responses to Violence in Mexico City', in R. K. Lippert and K. Walby (eds), *Policing Cities. Urban Securitization and Regulation in a Twenty-First Century World*, Abingdon: Routledge, pp. 113–129.

DDLDB (Diario de los debates de la Asamblea Legislativa del Distrito Federal) (1999) *Segundo periodo ordinario de sesiones del segundo año de ejercicio*, Mexico City: Asamblea Legislativa del Distrito Federal.

Denissen, I. (2009) 'New Forms of Political Inclusion: Competitive Clientelism', in Dutch Ministry of Foreign Affairs (ed.), *Quality and Effec-

tiveness: A Rich Menu for the Poor – Food for Thought on Effective Aid Policies, The Hague: Dutch Ministry of Foreign Affairs, available at www.minbuza.nl/en/appendices/key-topics/the-essays.html

Denyer Willis, G. (2015) *The Killing Consensus. Police, Organized Crime, and the Regulation of Life and Death in Urban Brazil*, Berkeley CA: University of California Press.

Dezalay, Y. and B. G. Garth (2002) *The Internationalization of Palace Wars. Lawyers, Economists, and the Contest to Transform Latin American States*, Chicago, IL: Chicago University Press.

Dezalay, Y. and B. G. Garth (2011) 'Hegemonic Battles, Professional Rivalries, and the International Division of Labor in the Market for the Import and Export of State-Governing Expertise', *International Political Sociology*, 5(3): 276–293.

Eckstein, S. (1988) *The Poverty of Revolution: The State and the Urban Poor in Mexico*, Princeton, NJ: Princeton University Press.

El Universal (2007a) 'Encuentra CDHDF violaciones en procesos de expropiación', 26 March.

El Universal (2007b) 'Prevé GDF reacción violenta por expropiación en Tepito', 24 February.

El Universal (2007c) 'Construyen "Tepiplaya" para protestar obras inconclusas', 25 April.

El Universal (2008) 'Confirma CDHDF insuficiencia de personal en juzgados cívicos', 19 December.

El Universal (2009) 'Sexoservidoras: policías nos acosan y piden dinero', 12 July.

El Universal (2010) 'Tepito abre una oficina en China', 10 January.

El Universal (2013) Endurece ALDF penas para delitos durante marchas, 19 November.

Fernández Muñoz, E. (2008) *Los usos políticos de la pobreza. Política social y clientelismo electoral en la alternancia*, Toluca: El Colegio Mexiquense.

Fischer, B. (2014) 'A Century in the Present Tense: Crisis, Politics, and the Intellectual History of Brazil's Informal Cities', in B. Fischer, B. McCann and J. Auyero (eds) Cities From Scratch: Poverty and Informality in Urban Latin America, Durham, NC: Duke University Press, pp. 9–67.

Focus (Focus On Human Rights in Mexico) (2004) 'Lynchings: A Clear Symptom of the Government's Failure to Administer Justice'. Mexico City: Miguel Augustín Pro Juárez Human Rights Centre.

Fondevila, G. (2011) 'Madrinas: Snitching/Para-Policing and the Illegal Support of Police Work in Mexico', *Police Practice and Research*, 12(3): 223–234.

Fox, J. A. (1994) 'The Difficult Transition from Clientelism to Citizenship: Lessons from Mexico', *World Politics*, 46(2): 151–184.

Fox, J. A. (2012) 'State Power and Clientelism: Eight Propositions for Discussion', in T. Hilgers (ed.), *Clientelism and Everyday Latin American Politics*, Basingstoke: Palgrave Macmillan, pp. 187–212.

Fraser, N. (1990) 'Rethinking the Public Sphere: A Contribution to the Critique of Actually Existing Democracy', *Social Text*, 25(26): 56–80.

Fuentes Díaz, A. (2005) 'Subalternidad v violencia colectiva en México y Guatemala', *Fermentum* 16(46): 415–28.

Gaceta Oficial del Distrito Federal (2007) *Décima séptima época*. 14 Febrero 2007. Mexico City: Gobierno del Distrito Federal.

Garces, C. (2014) 'Ecuador's 'Black Site': On Prison Securitization and its Zones of Legal Silence', *Focaal: Journal of Global and Historical Anthropology*, 68: 18–34.

Garza, J. A. (2007) *The Imagined Underworld. Sex, Crime and Vice in Porfirian Mexico City*, Lincoln, NE: University of Nebraska Press.

Gledhill, J. (2015) *The New War on the Poor. The Production of Insecurity in Latin America*, London: Zed Books.

Goldstein, D. M. (2003) '"In Our Own Hands": Lynching, Justice, and the Law in Bolivia'. *American Ethnologist*, 30(1): 22–43.

Goldstein, D. M. (2004) *The Spectacular City: Violence and Performance in Urban Bolivia*, Durham, NC: Duke University Press.

Goldstein, D. M. (2005) 'Flexible Justice: Neoliberal Violence and "Self-Help" Security in Bolivia', *Critique of Anthropology*, 25(4): 389–411.

Goldstein, D. M. (2012) *Outlawed: Between Security and Rights in a Bolivian City*, Durham, NC: Duke University Press.

González Ruiz, S., E. López Portillo and A. Yáñez R. (1994) *Seguridad pública en México: problemas perspectivas y propuestas*, Mexico City: UNAM.

Grindle, M. S. (1977) *Bureaucrats, Politicians, and Peasants in Mexico*, Berkeley CA: University of California Press.

Guerrien, M. (2004) *L'enfance agitée d'une mégapole. Transition urbaine et fragmentation de l'espace dans la vallée de Mexico*. PhD Thesis, Ecole des Hautes Études en Sciences Sociales, Paris.

Gutierrez Rivera (2013) *Territories of Violence. State, Marginal Youth, and Pubilc Security in Honduras*, Basingstoke: Palgrave Macmillan.

Gutman, M. C. (2006) *The Romance of Democracy. Compliant Defiance in Contemporary Mexico*, Berkeley, CA: University of California Press.

Harvey, D. (2000) *Spaces of Hope*, Berkeley, CA: University of California Press.

Harvey, D. (2006) *Spaces of Global Capitalism. Towards a Theory of Uneven Geographical Development*, London: Verso

Hathazay, P. and M.-M. Müller (2016) 'The Rebirth of the Prison in Latin America: Determinants, Regimes and Social Effects,' *Crime, Law & Social Change* 65(3): 113-135.

Hathazy, P. (2013) '(Re)Shaping the Neoliberal Leviathan: The Politics of Penality and Welfare in Argentina, Chile and Peru', *European Review of Latin American and Caribbean Studies*, 95: 5–26.

Heigl, M. C. (2011) 'Social Conflict and Competing State Projects in the Semi-periphery: A Strategic-relational Analysis of the Transformation of the Mexican State into an Internationalized Competition State', *Antipode*, 43(1): 129–148.

Hernández, A. (2008) 'The Vita-*Migas* of Tepito', *Ethnology*, 47(2): 89–93.

Herzog, L. A. (2003) 'La política, el diseño y el espacio público en la Ciudad de México y en Barcelona', in N. García Canclini (ed.), *Reabrir espacios Públicos. Políticas Culturales y ciudadanía*, Mexico City: UAM/Plaza y Valdés, pp. 267–303.

Hilgers, T. (2008) 'Causes and Consequences of Political Clientelism: Mexico's PRD in Comparative Perspective', *Latin American Politics and Society*, 50(4): 123–153.

Hilgers, T. (2009) 'Who is Using Whom? Clientelism from the Client's Perspective', *Journal of Iberian and Latin American Research*, 15(1): 51–76.

Hilgers, T. (2011) 'La relation complexe entre clientélisme et démocratie', *politique et Sociétés*, 30: 123–146.

Hilgers, T. (ed.) (2012) *Clientelism in Everyday Latin American Politics*, Basingstoke: Palgrave Macmillan.

Hochmüller, M. and M.-M. Müller (2014) 'Encountering Knowledge Production: The International Crisis Group and the Making of Mexico's Security Crisis', *Third World Quarterly*, 35(4): 705–722.

Hochmüller, M. and M.-M. Müller (2016) 'Locating Guatemala in Global Counterinsurgency', *Globalizations*, 13(1): 94-109.

HRW (Human Rights Watch) (1991) *Prison Conditions in Mexico*, New York: Human Rights Watch.

Hudson, J. R. and A. Medrano (2013) 'Nation-State Global City Tensions in Social Policy: The Case of Mexico City's Rising Social City-Citizenship', *Journal of International and Comparative Social Policy*, 23(1): 1–14.

ICESI (Instituto Ciudadano de Estudios Sobre la Inseguridad A.C.) (2008) 'Encuesta Nacional sobre Inseguridad (ENSI-5)', www.icesi.org.mx/documentos/propuestas/cuadernos_icesi.pdf [accessed 2 March 2009].

ICESI (Instituto Ciudadano de Estudios Sobre la Inseguridad A.C.), 'Encuesta Nacional sobre Inseguridad (ENSI-7)", (2010) www.icesi.org.mx/documentos/encuestas/encuestasNacionales/ENSI-7_resultados_nacional_y_por_entidades_federativas.pdf [accessed 19 January 2012].

Igreja Lemos, R. (2004) 'Derecho y diferencia étnica: La impartición de justicia hacia los indígenas migrantes en la Ciudad de México', in M. Teresa Sierra (ed.) *Haciendo justicia. Integralidad, derecho y género en regiones indígenas*, Mexico City: Miguel Ángl de Porrúa: 409–474.

ILO (International Labour Organization) (2014) *Informal Employment in Mexico: Current Situation, Policies and Challenges*, Lima: International Labour Organization, Regional Office for Latin America and the Caribbean.

INEGI (Instituto Nacional de Estadística y Geografía) (2004) *Delimitación de las zonas metropolitanas de México*, Mexico City: INEGI.

INEGI (Instituto Nacional de Estadística y Geografía) (2011) *Panorama sociodemográfico del Distrito Federal*, Mexico City: INEGI.

Iturralde, M. (2010) 'Democracies without Citizenship: Crime and Punishment in Latin America', *New Criminal Law Review*, 13(2): 309–332.

Jacobs, J. (1961) *The Death and Life of Great American Cities*, New York: Vintage Books.

Jensen, S. (2007) 'Policing Nkomazi: Crime, Masculinity and Generational Conflicts', in D. Pratten and A. Seen (eds) *Global Vigilantes*, London: Hurst: 47–68.

Jiménez Ornelas, R. A. and M. Moreno Alva (2007) 'Reto fundamental: la seguridad pública', in L. González Placencia, J. L. Arce Aguilar and M. Álvarez (eds), *Once aproximaciones empíricas al estudio de la inseguridad. Once estudios en materia de seguridad ciudadana en México*, Mexico City: Miguel Ángel Porrúa, pp. 197–210.

Kanai, M. and I. Ortega-Alcázar (2009) 'The Prospects for Progressive Culture-Led Urban Regeneration in Latin America: Cases From Mexico City and Buenos Aires', *International Journal of Urban and Regional Research*, 33(2): 483–501.

Kanitscheider, S. (2002) 'Condominios und fraccionamientos cerrados in Mexiko-Stadt. Sozialräumliche Segregation am Beispiel abgesperrter Wohnviertel', *Geographica Helvetica*, 57(4): 253–263.

Keck, M. and K. Sikkink (1998) *Activists beyond Borders: Advocacy Networks in International Politics*, Ithaca, NY: Cornell University Press.

Kenny, P. and M. Serrano (eds) (2012) *Mexico's Security Failure: Collapse into Criminal Violence*, London: Routledge.

Koonings, K. (2012) 'New Violence, Insecurity, and the State: Comparative Reflections on Latin America and Mexico', in W. Pansters (ed.), *Violence Coercion, and State-Making in Twentieth-Century Mexico*, Palo Alto CA: Stanford University Press, pp. 255–278.

Koonings, K. and D. Kruijt (1999) 'Introduction: Violence and Fear in Latin America', in Koonings, K. and D. Kruijt (eds), *Societies of Fear. The Legacy of Civil War, Violence and Terror in Latin America*, London: Zed Books, pp. 1–30.

Koonings, K. and D. Kruijt (2007) 'Introduction: The Duality of Latin American Cityscapes', in K. Koonings and D. Kruijt (eds), *Fractured Cities. Social Exclusion, Urban Violence & Contested Spaces in Latin America*, London: Zed Books, pp. 7–22.

Koonings, K. and D. Kruijt (2015a) 'Urban Fragility and Resilience in Latin America: Conceptual Approaches and Contemporary Patterns', in K. Koonings and D. Kruijt (eds) *Violence and Resilience in Latin American Cities*, London: Zed Books, pp. 1–29.

Koonings, K. and D. Kruijt (2015b) 'Exclusion, Violence and Resilience in Five Latin American Megacities: A Comparison of Buenos Aires, Lima, Mexico City, Rio de Janeiro and São Paulo', in K. Koonings and D. Kruijt (eds) *Violence and Resilience in Latin American Cities*, London: Zed Books, pp. 30–52.

La Jornada (1997) 'Cero tolerancia contra el hampa, dice el encargado de la Judicial', December 17.

La Jornada (2004a) 'La marcha del 27', 21 June.

La Jornada (2004b) 'Del acarreo yuppie al pueblo raso, cada quien con su bandera', 28 June.

La Jornada (2004c) 'Celebra aprobación de la Ley de Justicia Cívica', 30 April.

La Jornada (2007a) 'Propondrá Ebrard legislación sobre "extinción de dominio', 16 February.

La Jornada (2007b) 'Tepiplaya', 25 April.

La Jornada (2008) 'En tres puntos de La Merced se concentran bodegas adaptadas como hoteles de paso', 16 May.

La Jornada (2009) 'Los de Abajo. Amenazas de activistas en La Merced', 28 March.

La Jornada (2012) 'Propone Ebrard 30 años de cárcel a quien perturbe la paz social', 1 November.

Levitsky, S. and K. M. Roberts (eds) (2011) *The Resurgence of the Left in Latin America*, Baltimore, MD: Johns Hopkins University Press.

Levitsky, S. and M. V. Murillo (2005) 'Conclusion: Theorizing about Weak Institutions: Lessons from the Argentine Case', in S. Levitsky and M.V. Murillo (eds) *Argentine Democracy. The Politics of Institutional Weakness*, University Park, PA: Pennsylvania University Press.

Lippert, R. K. and K. Walby (eds) (2013) *Policing Cities: Urban Securitization and Regulation in a 21st Century World*, Abingdon: Routledge.

López-Montiel, A. G. (2000) 'The Military, Political Power, and Police Relations in Mexico City', *Latin American Perspectives*, 27(2): 79–94.

Low, S. 'Towards a Theory of Urban Fragmentation: A Cross-Cultural Analysis of Fear, Privatization, and the State', *Cybergeo: European Journal of Geography* (online). Available at: http://cybergeo.revues.org/3207 [accessed, 22 January 2016].

Luccisano, L. and L. Macdonald (2013) 'Guns and Butter: Social Policy, Semi-Clientelism, and Efforts to Reduce Violence in Mexico City'. Paper prepared for the Wokrshop 'Clientelism and Violence in Subnational Latin American Politics', Carleton University, Ottawa, 13–14 December 2013.

Magaloni, B. (2006) *Voting for Autocracy: Hegemonic Party Survival and its Demise in Mexico City*, New York: Cambridge University Press.

Marek, J. (2010) 'Desde acá – Tepito, barrio en la Ciudad de México', *Revista del CESLA*, 2(13): 231–542.

Martínez de Murguía, B. (1999) *La Policía en México: ¿Orden social o criminalidad?*, Mexico City: Planeta.

Mendieta Jiménez, E. (2006) 'Seguridad pública y seguridad privada ¿complementarias o antagónicas?' in J. P. Peñaloza (ed.), *Seguridad pública. Voces diversas en un enfoque multidisciplinario*, Mexico City: Editorial Porrúa, pp. 409–436.

Merry, S. E. (2005) *Human Rights and Gender Violence. Translating International Law Into Local Justice*, Chicago, IL: University of Chicago Press.

Mitchell, K. and K. Beckett (2008) 'Securing the Global City: Crime, Consulting, Risk, and Ratings in the Production of Urban Space', *Indiana Journal of Global Legal Studies*, 15(1): 75–99.

Moe, L. W. (2016). The Strange Wars of Liberal Peace: Hybridity, Complexity and the Governing Rationalities of Counterinsurgency in Somalia, *Peacebuilding* 4(1): 99-117.

Moe, L. W. and M.-M. Müller (2015) 'Resilience as Warfare: Interventions and the Militarization of the Social in Haiti and Somalia', *Kriminologisches Journal*, 47(4): 279–296.

Moreira Alves, M. H. and P. Evanson (eds) (2011) *Living in the Crossfire. Favela Residents, Drug Dealers, and Police Violence in Rio de Janeiro*, Temple, PA: Temple University Press.

Morton, A. D. (2012) 'The War on Drugs in Mexico: A Failed State?', *Third World Quarterly*, 33(9): 1631–1645.

Mountz, A. and W. Curran (2009) 'Policing in Drag. Giuliani goes Global with the Illusion of Control', *Geoforum*, 40(6): 1033–1040.

Müller, F. (2015) *The Global City and its Other. Decentering Urban Informality in and from Mexico City*, Berlin: Edition Tranvia.

Müller, M.-M. (2009a) 'Wenn "Null Toleranz" und "Zerbrochene Fensterscheiben" auf Reisen gehen: Globalisierung und die Restrukturierung des historischen Zentrums in Mexiko-Stadt', *Kriminologisches Journal*, 41(2): 82–99.

Müller, M.-M. (2009b) 'The Struggle over Human Rights in Mexico', in K. Hoffman Holland (ed.), *Ethics and Human Rights in a Globalized World*, Tübingen: Mohr-Siebeck.

Müller, M.-M (2010a) 'Community Policing in Latin America: Lessons from Mexico City', *European Review of Latin American and Caribbean Studies*, 88: 21–37.

Müller, M.-M. (2010b) 'Private Security and the State in Latin America: The Case of Mexico City'. *Brazilian Political Science Review*, 4(1): 131–154.

Müller, M.-M. (2012a) 'The Rise of the Penal State in Latin America', *Contemporary Justice Review*, 15(1): 57–76.

Müller, M.-M. (2012b) 'The Universal and the Particular in Latin American Penal State Formation', in P. Squires and J. Lea (eds), *Criminalisation and Advanced Marginality. Critically Exploring the Work of Loïc Wacquant*, Bristol: Policy Press, pp. 195–216.

Müller, M.-M. (2012c) *Public Security in the Negotiated State. Policing in Latin America and Beyond*, Basingstoke: Palgrave Macmillan.

Müller, M.-M. (2012d) 'Addressing an Ambivalent Relationship: Policing and the Urban Poor in Mexico City', *Journal of Latin American Studies*, 44(2): 319–345.

Müller, M.-M. (2013a) '"Public" Security and Patron Client Exchanges in Latin America', *Government & Opposition*, 48(4): 548–69.

Müller, M.-M. (2013b) 'The Clientelist Bases of Police Violence in Mexico City'. Paper prepared for the Workshop 'Clientelism and Violence in Subnational Latin American Politics', Carleton University, Ottawa, 13–14 December 2013.

Müller, M.-M. (2014) 'De-Monopolizing the Bureaucratic Field: Internationalization Strategies and the Transnationalization of Security Governance in Mexico City', *Alternatives: Global, Local, Political*, 39(1): 37–54.

Müller, M.-M. (2015) 'Punitive Entanglements: The "War on Gangs" and the Making of a Transnational Penal Apparatus in the Americas', *Geopolitics*, 20(3): 696–727.

Müller, M.-M. (2016a) 'Penalizing Democracy: Punitive Politics in Neoliberal Mexico', *Crime, Law & Social Change* 65(3): 227-249.

Müller, M.-M. (2016b) 'Entangled Pacifications: Peacekeeping, Policing and Counterinsurgency in Port-au-Prince and Rio de Janeiro', in J. Hönke and M.-M. Müller (eds), *The Global Making of Policing. Postcolonial Perspectives*, London: Routledge, pp. 77-95.

Naval, C. (2006) *Irregularidades, abusos de poder y maltratos en el Distrito Federal. Relación de los agentes policiales y del ministerio público con la población*, Mexico City: Fundar A.C.

Neocleous, M. (2008) *Critique of Security*, Edinburgh: Edinburgh University Press.

O'Grady, H. (2005) *Woman's Relationship with Herself: Gender, Foucault, and Therapy*, London: Routledge.

O'Neill, K. L. and K. Thomas (eds) (2011) *Securing the City: Neoliberalism, Space, and Insecurity in Postwar Guatemala*, Durham, NC: Duke University Press.

OECD (Organisation for Economic Co-operation and Development) (2013) *OECD Economic Surveys: Mexico 2013*, Paris: OECD Publishing.

Pansters, W. (2012a) 'Zones of State-Making: Violence, Coercion, and Hegemony in Twentieth-Century Mexico', in W. Pansters (ed.), *Violence, Coercion, and State-Making in Twentieth-Century Mexico. The Other Half of the Centaur*, Palo Alto CA: Stanford University Press, pp. 3–42.

Pansters, W. (ed.) (2012b). *Violence, Coercion, and State-Making in Twentieth-Century Mexico. The Other Half of the Centaur*, Palo Alto CA: Stanford University Press.

Pansters, W. and H. Castillo Berthier (2007) 'Mexico City', in K. Koonings and D. Kruijt (eds), *Fractured Cities. Social Exclusion, Urban Violence and Contested Spaces in Latin America*, London: Zed Books, pp. 36–56.

Parnreiter, C. (2002) 'Mexico: The Making of a Global City', in S. Sassen (ed.), *Global Networks, Linked Cities*, New York: Routledge, pp. 145–182.

Pearce, J. (2010) 'Perverse State Formation and Securitized Democracy in Latin America', *Democratization*, 17(2): 286–306.

Peck, J., N. Theodore and N. Brenner (2009) 'Neoliberal Urbanism: Models, Moments, Mutations', *SAIS Review*, 29(1): 49–66.

Perlman, J. (2010) *Favela: Four Decades of Living on the Edge in Rio de Janeiro*, Oxford: Oxford University Press.

PGDDF (Programa General de Desarrollo del Distrito Federal) (2000) 2001–2006. Mexico City: Gobierno del Distrito Federal.

Piccato, P. (2001) *City of Suspects. Crime in Mexico City, 1900-1931*, Durham, NC: Duke University Press.

Piccato, P. (2005) 'Communities and Crime in Mexico City', *Delaware Review of Latin American Studies*, 6/1. Available at: www.udel.edu/LAS/Vol6-1Piccato.html [accessed 17 February 2007].

Piccato, P. (2007) 'A Historical Perspective on Crime in Twentieth-Century Mexico City', in W. A. Cornelius and D. A. Shirk (eds), *Reforming the Administration of Justice in Mexico*, Notre Dame, IN: University of Notre Dame Press, pp. 65–90.

Plehwe, D. (2001) 'Neoliberale Ideen aus der nationalen Peripherie ins Zentrum gerückt', *Utopie kreativ*, 129/130: 634–643.

Portes, A. and B. R. Roberts (2005) 'The Free-Market City: Latin American Urbanization in the Years of the Neoliberal Experiment', *Studies in Comparative International Development*, 40(1): 43–82.

Presidencia de la República (2012) *Sexto informe de gobierno*, Mexico City: Poder Ejecutivo.

ProDh (Centro de Derechos Humanos Miguel Augustín Pro Juárez A.C.) (2001) *Justicia por propia mano*, Mexico City.

Programa Parcial de Desarrollo Urbano Centro Histórico (PPDUCH) (2000) *Gaceta Oficial del Distrito Federal*, 7 September 2000, Mexico City: Gobierno del Distrito Federal.

Rajkovic, N. M. (2010) '"Global Law" and Governmentality: Reconceptualizing the "Rule of Law" as "Rule Through Law"', *European Journal of International Relations*, 18(1), pp. 29–52.

Ramírez Cuevas, J. (2004) 'La Ley de Talión no es costumbre indígena. Cuando una comunidad se convierte en turba' 363°, 5.12.2004.

Ramírez Cuevas, J. (2005) 'La furia del México roto y excluido', *Masiosare*, 369: 1–5.

Reames, B. N. (2008) 'Paths to Fairness, Effectiveness, and Democratic Policing in Mexico', in R. Haberfeld and I. Cerrah (eds) *Comparative Policing. The Struggle for Democratization*, Los Angeles, CA: Sage, pp. 97–120.

Revista Contralínea (2008) 'La calle es de quien la trabaja', 15 February.

Roberts, K. M. (2014) *Changing Course in Latin America. Party Systems in the Neoliberal Era*, Cambridge: Cambridge University Press.

Ross, J. (2003) 'Guns, trade and "Control"', *NACLA Report on the Americas*, 37(2): 18–19.

Ruiz Ortega, H. (2006) *Crecimiento de la población penitenciaria*, Mexico City: Subsecretaría del sistema penitenciaria. Available at: [accessed 13 September 2012].

Sadler, L. R. (2000) 'The Historical Dynamics of Smuggling in the U.S.-Mexican Border Region, 1550-1998', in J. Bailey and R. Godson (eds), *Organized Crime and Democratic Governability. Mexico and the U.S.-Mexican Borderlands*, Pittsburgh, PA: University of Pittsburgh Press, pp. 161–176.

Schild, V. (2015) 'Securing Citizens and Entrenching Inequalities: The Gendered, Neoliberalized Latin American State', desiguALdades.net *Working Paper Series 83*, Berlin: desiguALdades.net International Research Network on Interdependent Inequalities in Latin America.

Schlefer, J. (2008) *Palace Politics: How the Ruling Party Brought Crisis to Mexico*, Austin, TX: University of Texas.

Scott, J. (1972) 'Patron–Client Politics and Political Change in Southeast Asia', *American Political Science Review*, 66(1): 91–113.

Scott, J. C. (1990) *Domination and the Arts of Resistance: Hidden Transcripts*, New Haven, CT: Yale University Press.

Sierra, M. T. (2005) 'The Revival of Indigenous Justice in Mexico: Challenges for Human Rights and the State', *Political and Legal Anthropology Review*, 28(1): 52–72.

Silva, C. (2007) 'Police Abuse in Mexico City', in W. A. Cornelius and D. A. Shirk (eds) *Reforming the Administration of Justice in Mexico*, Notre Dame, IN: University of Notre Dame Press, pp. 175–194.

Silvestre, G. (2016) 'Local Consequences of the Prison Policies in the state of São Paulo, Brazil: A Case Study of the Town of Itirapina', *Crime, Law and Social Change*, 65(3): 269-285.

Smith, N. (1996) *New Urban Frontier: Gentrification and the Revanchist City*. London: Routledge.

Smith. N. (2005) 'El redimensionamiento de las ciudades: la globalización y el urbanismo neoliberal,' in D. Harvey and N. Smith, *Capital financiero, propiedad inmobilaria y cultura*, Barcelona: Universitat Autònoma de Barcelona, pp. 59–78

Soederberg, S. (2010) 'The Mexican Competition State and the Paradoxes of Managed Neo-liberal Development',', *Policy Studies*, 31(1): 77–94.

SSPDF (Secretaría de Seguridad Pública del Distrito Federal) (2003) *Reporte Giuliani SSP*. Mexico City: SSPDF.

SSPDF (Secretaría de Seguridad Pública del Distrito Federal) (2006a) Memoria Institucional: 2000–2006. Mexico City: SSPDF.

SSPDF (Secretaría de Seguridad Pública del Distrito Federal) (2006b) Informe Sexenal de Actividades de la Secretaría de Seguridad Pública del Distrito Federal. Mexico City: SSPDF.

SSPDF (Secretaría de Seguridad Pública del Distrito Federal) (2008) *Comunicado 602/08*, Mexico City: SSPDF.

SSPDF (Secretaría de Seguridad Pública del Distrito Federal) (2009) 'Seguridad: A TU ALCANCE', leaflet distributed by local police department, Mexico City.

Stanley, R. (2010) '"Living in a Jungle:" State Violence and Perceptions of Democracy in Buenos Aires', in E. D. Arias and D. M. Goldstein (eds), *Violent Democracies in Latin America*, Durham, NC: Duke University Press, pp. 133–160.

Stanley, R., R. Figari-Layus and M.-M. Müller (2009) *The Transnationalisation of Public Security Governance: Evidence from Argentina and Mexico*, unpublished manuscript, Berlin.

Stokes, S. C. (2007) 'Political Clientelism', in S. C. Stokes and B. Carles (eds), *The Oxford Handbook of Comparative Politics*, Oxford: Oxford University Press: pp. 604–627.

Swanson, K. (2007) 'Revanchist Urbanism Heads South: The Regulation of Indigenous Beggars and Street Vendors in Ecuador', *Antipode*, 39(4): 708–728.

Swanson, K. (2010) *Begging as a Path to Progress. Indigenous Women and Children and the Struggle for Ecuador's Urban Spaces*, Athens, GA: University of Georgia Press.

Swanson, K. (2013) 'Zero Tolerance in Latin America: Punitive Paradox in Urban Policy Mobilities', *Urban Geography*, 34(7): 972–988.

Tello, N. (2012) 'Police Reforms: The Voice of Police and Residents in Mexico City', *Policing and Society*, 22(1): 14–27.

Thomas K., K. L. O'Neill and T. Offit (2011) 'An Introduction', in K. L. O'Neill and K. Thomas (eds), *Securing the City: Neoliberalism, Space, and Insecurity in Postwar Guatemala*, Durham, NC: Duke University Press, pp. 1–21.

Tironi, M. and J. Barandiarán (2014) 'Neoliberalism as Political Technology: Expertise, Energy and Democracy in Chile', in E. Medina, I. da Costa Marques and C. Holmes (eds), *Beyond Imported Magic: Essays on Science, Technology, and Society in Latin America*. Cambridge, MA: MIT Press, pp. 305–331.

Treverton, G. F., C. Matthies, K. J. Cunningham, J. Goulka, G. Ridgeway and A. Wong (2009) *Film Piracy, Organized Crime, and Terrorism. Appendixes A, B, and C*, Santa Monica, CA: RAND.

Uildriks, N. (2010) *Mexico's Unrule of Law. Implementing Human Rights in Police and Judicial Reform under Democratization*, Lanham, MA: Lexington Books.

Valenzuela Aguilar, A. (2013) 'Urban Surges: Power, Territory, and the Social Control of Space in Latin America', *Latin American Perspectives*, 40(5): 21–34

Vargas Hernández, J. G. and M. Reza Noruzi (2011) 'Theoretical Approaches to Shrinking Cities in Mexico', *International Journal of Business and Social Science*, 2(2): 86–91.

Vilas, C. M. (2001) '(In)justicia por mano propia: linchamientos en el México contemporáneo', *Revista Mexicana de Sociología*, 63(1): 131–60.

Villoro, J (2008) 'Horizontaler Schwindel. Mexiko Stadt als Diskurs', in A. Becker et al. (eds) *Verhandlungssache Mexiko Stadt. Umkämpfte Räume, Stadtaneignungen, imaginarios urbanos*, Berlin: b_books (metroZones 8): 27–42.

Vitale, A. S. (2008) *City of Disorder. How the Quality of Life Campaign Transformed New York Politics*, New York: New York University Press.

Vite Pérez, M. Á. (2001) 'Clientelismo político y exclusión social: el caso de Cuautepec', *Sociológica*, 16(47): 199–238.

Wacquant L (2007) 'Territorial Stigmatization in the Age of Advanced Marginality', *Thesis Eleven*, 91(1): 66–77.

Wacquant, L. (2008a) 'The Militarization of Urban Marginality: Lessons from the Brazilian Metropolis', *International Political Sociology*, 1(2): 56–64.

Wacquant, L. (2008b) *Urban Outcasts. A Comparative Sociology of Advanced Marginality*, Oxford: Polity Press.

Wacquant, L. (2008c) 'Relocating Gentrification: The Working Class, Science and the State in Recent Urban Research', *International Journal of Urban and Regional Research*, (32)1: 198-205.

Wacquant, L. (2009a) *Punishing the Poor. The Neoliberal Government of Social Insecurity*, Durham, NC: Duke University Press.

Wacquant, L. (2009b) *Prisons of Poverty. Expanded Edition*, Minnesota, MN: University of Minnesota Press.

Watt, P. and R. Zepeda (2012) *Drug War Mexico. Politics, Neoliberalism and Violence in the New Narcoeconomy*, London: Zed Books.

Wæver, O. (1995) 'Securitization and Desecuritization', in R. D. Lipschutz (ed.), *On Security*, New York: Columbia University Press, pp. 46–87.

Weber, R. (2002) Extracting Value from the City: Neoliberalism and Urban Redevelopment. *Antipode*, 34(3), 520–540.

Weyland, K. (2010) *Leftist Governments in Latin America: Successes and Shortcomings*, Cambridge, MA: Cambridge University Press.

Wigle, J. (2014) 'The "Graying" of "Green" Zones: Spatial Governance and Irregular Settlements in Xochimilco, Mexico City', *International Journal of Urban and Regional Research*, 38(2), 573–589.

Zapata Schaffeld, F. (2004) '¿Democratización o rearticulación del corporativismo? El caso de México', *Política*, 42: 13–40.

Zárate Hernández, J. E. J. (2005) 'Caciques and Leaders in the Era of Democracy', in A. Knight and W. Pansters (eds), *Caciquismo in Twentieth-Century Mexico*, London: Institute for the Study of the Americas, pp. 249–71.

Zaremberg, G. (2010) 'Hexágono versus árbol: casos atípicos en la organización del comercio informal en el Distrito Federal', *Perfiles Latinoamericanos*, 36: 154-155.

INDEX